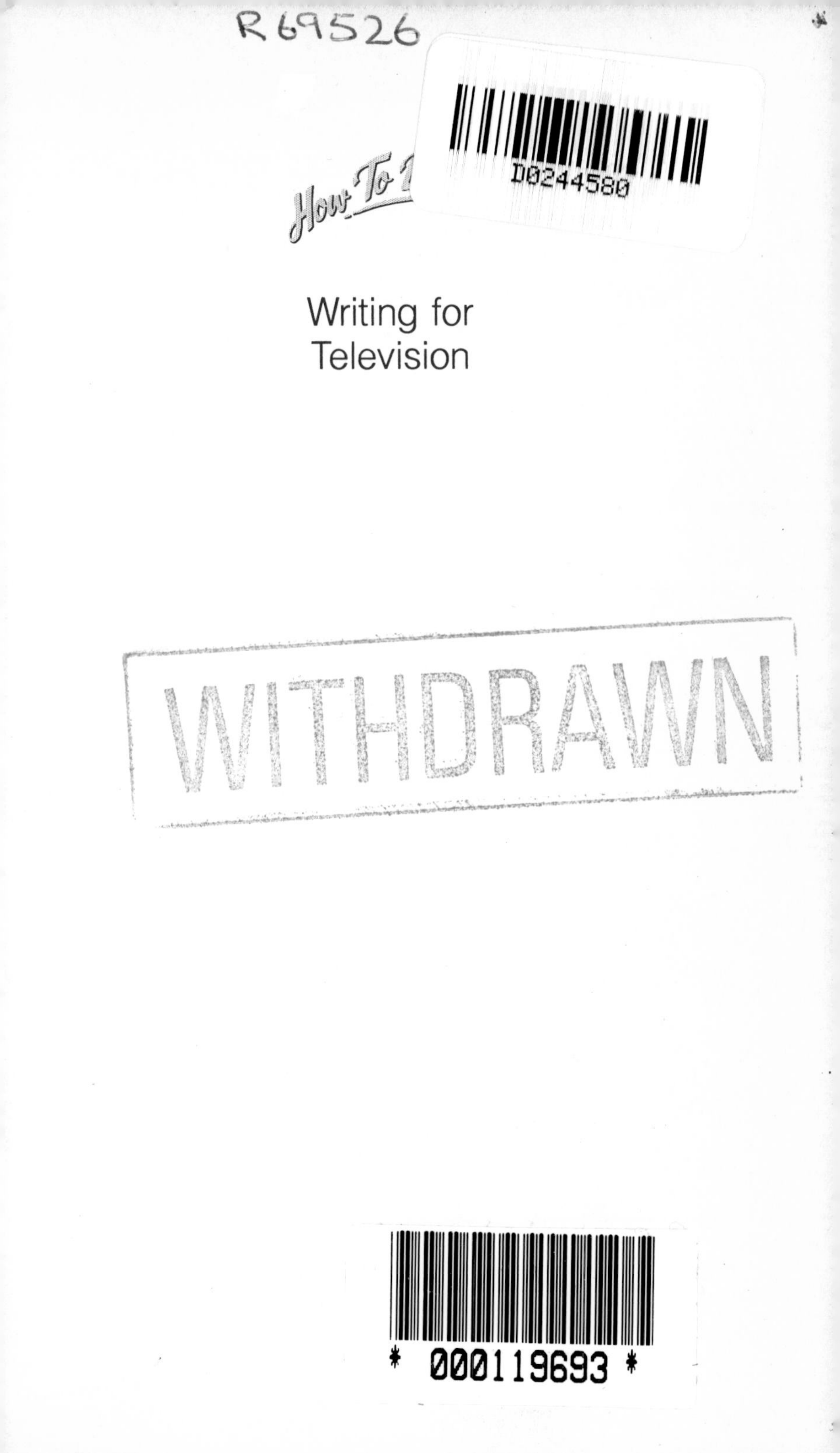

Writing for Television

Writing for Television

How to write and sell successful TV scripts

WILLIAM SMETHURST

3rd edition

How To Books

Published by How To Books Ltd,
3 Newtec Place, Magdalen Road,
Oxford OX4 1RE. United Kingdom.
Tel: (01865) 793806. Fax: (01865) 248780.
email: info@howtobooks.co.uk
http://www.howtobooks.co.uk

First edition 1992
Second edition 1998
Third edition 2000

British Library Cataloguing in Publication Data.
A catalogue record for this book is available from the British Library.

Cartoons by Mike Flanagan
Cover design by Shireen Nathoo Design
Cover image PhotoDisc

Produced for How To Books by Deer Park Productions
Typeset by PDQ Typesetting, Newcastle-under-Lyme
Printed and bound by Cromwell Press, Trowbridge, Wiltshire

Contents

List of Illustrations

The Opportunities

TELEVISION NEEDS *YOU*!

Television desperately needs new writers. It is a growth industry with an insatiable hunger for writing talent. There used to be just BBC 1. Now there are five terrestrial channels and a host of satellite providers. There used to be just *Coronation Street* (going back even further, if we're being pedantic, there used to be just *The Grove Family*). Now there is *Emmerdale* and *Eastenders* and *Brookside* and *Hollyoaks* for teenagers, and *Byker Grove*, and Channel 5's *Family Affairs*. All these programmes – and all the series like *Peak Practice*, *London's Burning*, *Casualty*, *Holby City*, *Heartbeat* – need script-writers, and scriptwriters are increasingly in short supply. A good new writer on *The Bill*? Word flies round the industry, and before you know it the writer concerned is doing an episode of *The Vice* and *The Bill* script editors are bitterly complaining about having their writers pinched.

There are simply not enough skilled writers to go round. Every year, as the big series limber up for production, script editors are sacked because they have failed to find the writing talent to script their programmes. Every year the BBC, ITV and Channel 4 devote resources to develop new, original comedy writing, in the hope of finding the next *Absolutely Fabulous* or *Men Behaving Badly*. And this leads to a great puzzle. A mystery, even, that would baffle an Inspector Morse, a Scully or a Mulder.

Why, if there is such a shortage of writers, do thousands of would-be writers constantly have their scripts rejected? Why is writing for television apparently so difficult?

SKILLS AND TECHNIQUES

The first truth, of course, is that writing any kind of drama – theatre, radio or television – is a skilled craft. It is something that can encompass genius. It is what Shakespeare did, and Ben Jonson, and Molière and Sheridan. It is an activity that requires not only facility with words and skill with structure, but an acute sensitivity regarding people and the way they behave.

A dramatist is an architect, who uses words and pictures instead of bricks and girders to construct an edifice in which every word has its proper place and serves its proper function. To do this skilfully requires techniques and disciplines that no new writer can be expected to know intuitively, but must learn.

WHAT THE AUDIENCE WANTS

A second truth is that television drama demands more of its writers than most other media. Every writer of fiction, be it books, stage plays or broadcast, is a storyteller, a weaver of tales. But television dramatists must do more than captivate an audience: they must captivate a *mass* audience. If you write a novel that explores the theological choices facing Chilean monks in the early 19th century you might, with luck, find a publisher somewhere willing to print a few copies. If your subject is utterly incomprehensible you might even win a major literary prize.

But this won't do for television. Television – on whatever level – is about entertainment. It may be entertainment realising high ambitions and cultural values (though when, we ask ourselves, did we last see one of those?) or entertainment that seeks only to please for a fleeting moment. But every television drama – however literary or demanding its subject – must aim to satisfy millions of people. 'Drama draws people together with its powerful emotions and irrestible storytelling,' says the BBC. Unless a new writer knows how to choose a subject and write with confidence, this might well appear to be to be a daunting task.

HIGH COST = HIGH RISK

The high cost of television drama is another factor working against the new writer. Single film dramas can cost well over a million pounds to make. An episode of a series drama like *Holby City* or *Heartbeat* costs more than half a million. Even the cost of a half-hour episode of a low-budget soap opera costs more than £80,000. A script editor has to be very brave to commission a new, inexperienced writer, however promising. Will the new writer be able to cope with technical problems? Will he be able to act on the notes he is given for a second draft? Will he be able to come up with re-writes? Huge amounts of money are at stake! The competitive edge of the channel against the opposition is at stake! More importantly, the script editor's job is at stake! The temptation is to go with the tried-and-trusted writer. He might be burnt-out and weary unto death, but he will at least deliver a script that is the right length, with the right number of characters, and the right number of scenes.

WORKING IN YOUR FAVOUR

Despite the obstacles, the opportunities are there waiting to be taken. Look at the factors operating in your favour:

- Television drama and situation comedy are expanding markets.
- Script editors are expected to find new writers. If they fail they risk being sacked. They are as eager to find you as you are to find them.
- Because there is no formal scriptwriter qualification, no 'script school' or college, all new writers start on the outside, and come from diverse and often unlikely backgrounds. A shop assistant in Barrow-in-Furness is just as likely to succeed as a film school graduate in London.
- Comedy writers are in such demand that the BBC has a script unit specifically devoted to finding new ideas and new writers for 30-minute situation comedies.
- The turnover in existing writers is high. Apart from the normal loss due to age and mortality, scriptwriters frequently turn to other areas of writing – novels, stage plays – or start up independent production companies and become producers. Others, sadly, find that their scripts are no longer the kind that is wanted.
- Most scripts by new writers are very poor. They are often handwritten, the dialogue dull, the stories repetitive and the plotting obvious. Spelling can be atrocious, and layout careless, with many crossings-out. The urge to write television drama is at its strongest amongst the socially maladjusted – people who cannot cope very well with real life, and seek to live through a fantasy world of their own making. People of low intelligence often aspire to write television drama. Semi-literates send in scripts – and all too often, the cynic might say, they are accepted. Ninety per cent of

scripts can be – and are – mentally dismissed after reading half a page.

- Few new writers know the type of script they should be writing, or even what to do with their script when they have written it.

HOW TO SUCCEED

In the first place you must write a script that you can show as an example of your writing skills. This script may never be made into a programme – but that doesn't matter, even though it is made with blood, sweat and tears, and is the joy and pride of your life. This script is your CV. Its purpose is to impress script editors, agents and producers. You might be lucky and sell it for production, but it will have done its job brilliantly if it gets you a commission to write an episode of a series drama like *Casualty*, or a soap like *Emmerdale*, or an invitation to join an ITV sitcom workshop.

To impress and excite your script must:

- be original in concept
- be well constructed
- be confidently plotted
- have good dialogue
- have good characterisation
- be professionally presented.

In the second place you must learn how to sell your script – and thus sell yourself as a writer. To do this you will need to know:

- the kind of drama that television script editors are looking for
- the programmes that are actively looking for new writers
- how to get your script read by the only people that matter: those with the power to commission you to write.

This book is designed to help you to achieve all of these aims. Its first part gives you professional hints on how to write your script – tips that producers, agents and script editors would give you themselves if they had the time. Its second part gives you the vital inside information you need actually to sell yourself as a writer.

THE REWARDS

In the coming months there will be many, many writers who receive rejection letters. But somewhere there will be a writer – perhaps on the point of giving up hope – who answers the phone one dull, dreary morning and finds himself or herself being told something on the lines of: 'Brilliant script! We're going ahead with it straight away. Contracts department will be on to you about the fee. Can we have lunch tomorrow to talk about casting? We thought of Nicole Kidman for the main role, but we'd like your opinion so I've asked her to lunch as well . . . .'

Perhaps that writer will be you?

> There are two struggles: the struggle to write something good and the struggle to get it read. You have to attack both with single-minded persistence.
>
> (Christopher McQuarrie, writer of *The Usual Suspects*)

1

The Basics

MAKING A START

Whether you are interested in writing soap operas like *Eastenders*, or series dramas like *Heartbeat*, or serials in the tradition of *Sex, Chips and Rock'n Roll* or – going back a bit – *The Beiderbecke Affair* (the BBC would give anything for another *Beiderbecke Affair*), or sitcoms, or children's drama, you must first write an original television script that will impress script editors, producers, and TV agents with your ability as a writer.

Perhaps you already have a story in your head – some characters – a situation you think would be interesting. But how do you know if it is the sort of script that is wanted? Or how many characters and locations you ought to have? Or what is the right length?

Before we consider anything else, let us look at the basics. You have to be able to:

- write to an acceptable budget
- write to an acceptable length
- write the kind of drama that is wanted.

WRITING TO AN ACCEPTABLE BUDGET

This does not mean write to a *very low* budget. Despite the success of series like *The Royle Family* there is virtually no market for plays that involve a few people sitting in a room talking to each other. Today's television audience is blasé and easily bored. Producers who want high viewing figures (i.e. all of them) must try to provide the sort of action and location-shooting common to the cinema and to films made for the video market. Your script (unless it is a sitcom, see Chapter 9) needs to take us out and about, and include visual action. That said, you stand more chance of success if you give good 'production values' (i.e. provide interesting things to look at) at a relatively low cost. A play that takes advantage of the scenic beauty of a nature reserve – or the atmosphere of a seaside resort – is good. A play that requires location shooting in Paraguay and a jet liner crashing on the Houses of Parliament is bad. It is true that a small number of major dramas on BBC 2 and Channel 4 have multi-million pound feature-film budgets and can afford global locations, special effects, and large casts, but these films are almost invariably written by experienced writers.

WRITING TO AN ACCEPTABLE LENGTH

A full-length play should be aimed at a 60-minute or 90-minute slot. Alternatively, if you do not have an idea for a major drama, you could write a 10-minute play aimed at one of the series of 'shorts' (like *Jump Cats*) that run on Channel 4 and BBC 2.

Or if you have an idea for a serial – a four-part thriller, perhaps, or a drama series – you could write the first 60-minute episode (30 minutes if it is a serial for children) and a synopsis of the other episodes.

Situation comedy should always be written for a 30-minute slot.

- The advantage of the major 90-minute play is that it shows your ability to create characters, to write dialogue, to utilise the camera, and to handle your plot. It also shows that you are capable of sustained writing on a major theme.

- The advantage of the 60-minute play is that it shows the above virtues without requiring script editors to read as much. It also saves you printing and postage costs. And if you are writing about love lost/found/betrayed/young love it has a chance of being 'packaged' with others in a season of one-hour original love stories.

- The advantage of the 10-minute short is that it *is* short – and the script editor is therefore more likely actually to read it. It gives a glimpse of your talents without requiring labour and effort. Ten-minute shorts are, though, at the end of the day less convincing than a solid 90- or 60-minute play, and they are very difficult to write.

- The advantage of writing a 60-minute episode plus synopsis is that new ideas for serials and series are always in demand. If you are successful you will also have the right to script further episodes. And if your idea turns into a long-running series, you will earn a fee when other writers are commissioned on the basis of your format.

CHOOSING THE TYPE OF DRAMA

Some types of drama are in demand, and some are to be avoided by the new writer. Here we look at:

- contemporary drama
- historical drama
- plays about love and passion
- existing series and serials
- children's drama
- adaptations
- comedy drama
- situation comedy.

Contemporary drama

Both the BBC and Channel 4 are proud of the reputation for socially-aware drama they have built over the years, and most one-off television plays are about aspects of life today. A contemporary drama is therefore your safest bet. Even is your play is not bought, it will clearly show your talent with dialogue and characterisation. Such plays do not have to be grim and serious: many are written as love stories, comedies (see below), or as thrillers. If possible you should try to find an area of modern life that has not been exploited by others. An alternative is to write a play set in the recent past – a script or serial idea set in the 1960s or 1970s might well combine nostalgia with social interest.

Historical drama

Avoid. The market is small, the expense is great, most historical plays that reach the screen are adaptations (see below), and such projects generally originate with television companies who then cast around for a writer of experience. Another problem is that agents and script editors have difficulty assessing your skill with modern dialogue and characterisation when you are writing in a period setting.

Plays about love and passion

You will not go far wrong – in terms of subject matter – if you write the story of a human relationship set against a background of genuine contemporary life and involving contemporary social issues. You are thus combining what the viewers want to see with what the producers and directors want to do. Stories about love do not need to be soft and romantic. Recent plays in the strand *Love Bites* included a tale of single parents and drug addicts in Glasgow; a searing study of date rape (which included flash-forwards and split screens); and a bitter-sweet comedy about love between a black girl and a white boy.

Existing series and serials

Do not write a script for an existing programme like *Coronation Street* or *London's Burning*, even if you eventually want to write for the programme concerned. Most script editors will not even look at such scripts – they are interested in your own original talent, not in how well you copy what you see on the screen. If this is the market you are interested in, you should write an original contemporary 90-minute or 60-minute play, or a 60-minute episode for a serial or series of your own devising.

Children's drama

There's quite a lot of it, but the market for new writers is not as great as that for adult series and soaps. If this is your interest, your best bet is to devise a four-part or six-part serial, and write one episode together with synopses of the rest. It might not be accepted, but if your work is liked you will be encouraged and pointed in the direction of children's programmes that use outside writers. Children's drama is always low budget.

Adaptations

Although adaptations – particularly of classic novels or detective stories – are frequently made there is no opportunity here for the new writer.

Comedy drama

Very much in demand, but surprisingly little reaches the screen. *The Biederbecke Affair* is the classic, a more recent example being Marks and Gran's *Dirty Work*. ITV's rare single plays are often comedy drama. Writing realistic drama that also makes us laugh is not easy, but if your instincts take you in this direction there is a ready market.

Situation comedy

This is a big market, and both the BBC and ITV are actively looking for new writing talent. (See Chapter 9 for specific sitcom writing requirements, and Chapter 13, page 127, for information about what programme makers want.)

> BBC 1 needs drama events that are compulsive viewing on the night and talked about the next day. Our series should reflect the lives we lead (*Sunburn* and *Playing the Field*) or entice us into the worlds of others (*Silent Witness*).
>
> (BBC Commissioning Guide)

COMMON QUERIES

Is it true that you should always write about what you know about?

Generally speaking, yes. You need to avoid the more obvious situations (producers get sent a lot of dramas about students living in squalid flats from students living in squalid flats) but a doctor is more likely to write a hospital drama with conviction than is a solicitor. Script editors are impressed – or at the simplest level comforted – if they believe you are writing with inside knowledge. This does not mean that you can't write a drama about life on Mars unless you've been there; it does mean that you need to know about everything there is to know about Mars and the technology needed to sustain life on it.

The setting and subject do not have to be exotic. Stacking supermarket shelves at night might not be glamorous and exciting, but if you story is well told viewers will be fascinated to know the hidden dramas, rivalries, loves, and routines of supermarket life in the secret hours of the night.

Should my play be gritty and controversial?

Yes, if you have something you passionately want to say. Putting on gritty controversial plays makes producers feel that they are more than mere hacks in the entertainment business: it makes them feel that they are people of power and importance. In recent years we have seen television plays about drugs abuse, child abuse, incest, oppression within the family, homosexual oppression, rent boys, transvestites, lesbians (the first major television play about lesbians, *The Other Woman* by Watson Gould, was made in the early 1970s, but the subject is still regarded as adventurous), racial tension, prison scandals, mob violence, and corruption. Writers and producers have garnered a fruitful harvest from the fields of social discord, while studies in fidelity, honesty, loyalty, and the happy state of England have been as rare as golden eagles over Ealing.

But aren't gritty, controversial plays old hat?

Well, possibly. Children of the 1960s who went into television and became the *enfants terribles* of the 1970s, then rose to be commissioning editors and heads of drama, are now passing from the scene. Many of their successors are more concerned with property values in the Dordogne than social values in inner-city Britain. More gloomy still, from the point of view of a gritty controversialist, today's script editors (who are nearly all in their twenties) seem to be apolitical, though healthily interested in sex and money. A play about old-age pensioners dying of hypothermia might make their eyes glaze over, but give them a script called *Lesbian Snogs* and they'll sit up and take an interest right away.

Are some subjects more likely to be accepted than others?

Yes, but fashions can change very quickly. Just as an elusive thought-message tells all dress designers when to raise or lower hemlines, so all script editors are liable to decide they're sick of buggery plays just as you put the finishing touches to a cracking 90 minutes on the subject. There might be a leaning towards gritty northern plays ('gritty' maintains its popularity as a favoured television industry buzz word), or a fashion for witty, ironic plays set in the soft south, but by the time you catch the mood of the moment it will have changed, and although it only takes a second on your computer to change 'Swindon' to 'Scunthorpe' throughout your script, it is unlikely to help you sell it.

Recent fashions have included British political dramas, series dramas about soldiers and hospitals, and drama-documentaries in which real events have been fictionalised. But by the time these series appear on the screen it could be two years on from the time when they were commissioned.

Memorable single plays on the BBC in the 1990s included a reminiscence about a childhood in a family dominated by an Alsatian; an Alan Bennett play featuring the relationship between Anthony Blunt and the Queen; and a farce about inflation in post-Falklands Argentina.

What all these plays had was originality. They were fresh, and interesting, and different.

Are any drama slots specifically designed for new writing talent?
There haven't been recently, but who knows? BBC 1 tries to provide an 'opportunity to establish new writers' through low-cost drama series like *Doctors*. If Channel 4 has a new-writer slot it will give details on its online guide for independent producers (you can find it at www.channel4.co.uk). The BBC's comedy script unit actively seeks new sitcom writers, as do Channel 4 (Comedy Lab) and Carlton TV. Much of the search for comedy writing is now accessed online. (See Chapter 13 and Chapter 18.)

SUMMARY

- You should write a contemporary or near contemporary play, because this will demonstrate your ability with dialogue and characterisation.
- You should give us visual interest without too much cost.
- You should write either a) a full-length play, b) an episode plus a synopsis of further episodes, or c) a 10-minute short. A sitcom should be written for a 30-minute slot.
- You should try to find a setting that has not, to your knowledge, been used before, or give us an insight into an area of life we would not otherwise know about.

The BBC advises new writers to write the sort of play they themselves would like to see on the screen, choosing subjects from their own experience.

> The trick is to have a really good story and really good characters.
>
> (Lucy Gannon, *On Air*, BBC 2)

2

Story and Theme

WHAT IS YOUR PLAY *REALLY* ABOUT?

You have decided on:

- the length of script you are going to write
- the story you are going to tell
- the setting.

But what is your drama *actually going to be about*? Will it be about love – love betrayed, love that endures? Or about passion – passion that triumphs over all odds, passion that betrays and destroys? Or will it perhaps be about social justice – justice that triumphs, justice that is blind, justice that is abused?

The underlying subject of a play is sometimes known as **the theme** or **the premise**. It's what your play is about on a deeper level than the actual story. If an Elizabethan script editor had been asked to sum up *Othello* he might well have said 'jealousy'. Or he might have expanded slightly and said 'The study of a man destroyed by his own unreasoned jealousy.'

Single plays – particularly those of 60-minute or 90-minute duration – need to contain thoughts and ideas over and above the bricks and mortar of the actual story they tell. Producers and script editors know that *Othello* is more than a bit of chicanery that leads to a nasty domestic crisis. When they read your script they need to convince themselves that your play has something to tell us about life today, or about human nature.

Consider the following story idea.

> SAMMY SLIME is manager of the Hardtimes Residential Home for the Elderly. It is a council home but under the terms of 'opting-out' legislation he finds that he can claim state money for his residents without accounting for expenditure. Slowly he starves the residents, depriving them of food and heating and comfort until there is a dreary, debilitating reign of terror.

ELSIE, a courageous woman in her nineties tries to rally opposition to SLIME. But she is frail and catches pneumonia. We know that she will soon die unless SLIME is exposed.

The social services – council workers, overworked doctors – all fail to spot what is happening.

The other old folk long to help ELSIE, but are terrified of SLIME. Surely they will be shamed into helping her? They almost mount a rebellion – but not quite.

ELSIE's daughter is due from America. Will she turn up in time?

She doesn't. ELSIE dies. SLIME covers up evidence of malnutrition and gets a death certificate from a harassed young GP.

It seems that he can get away with everything. Until a dustman finds three dozen empty catfood tins outside the back door...

And the local paper gets hold of the story, and investigates.

Shorn of names like Slime and Hardtimes, used here to avoid libel risks inherent in realistic names (see **libel**, page 159), this is a sound enough, if rather gloomy narrative that would once have had considerable appeal to the BBC or Channel 4. In it we see a man in power ill-treating victims in his care. We see a victim try to oppose him. We wait for the social services or doctors to help the victim – and are horrified when they fail. We see a sudden ray of hope when the daughter is due from America! We see the hope dashed – and the victim die. We then see retribution from an unexpected but logical quarter.

This is the narrative – the superficial story. But it does not tell us how the play will actually be written, or what the play is actually about.

ANALYSING STORY OUTLINE

- Is it the story of Elsie, a woman who has perhaps been too timid during her life but who finds, when she is in her nineties, the strength to lead a struggle against oppression?

  The play will thus be a story of courage in extremity, and the triumph of the human spirit.

- Is it the story of Sammy Slime? Perhaps as a young man Sam went into his career with high ideals and a genuine desire to help his fellow human beings. Perhaps he makes his first 'profit' by mistake...then when he is not discovered, and when the old people do not notice, he is tempted to take a 'profit' yet again.

The play will thus be a study of how avarice consumes and destroys a man.

- Is it the story of the social services, underfunded for decades, with doctors that cannot cope, now inflicted with a form of 'privatisation' that leaves the people it ought to protect exposed to sordid profiteers?

Thus it will be a highly partisan political play, a trumpet call to the government to reverse the wicked capitalist policies it inherited and is still shamefully following.

The dramatist might say he wants to combine all these elements. The theme or premise might be: 'A searing exposure of neglect in our society, told through the battle of wills between a woman who finds courage she did not know she possessed, and a weak man who falls to temptation'.

Understanding your subject helps you to write your play. Even working it out in your head encourages you to probe deeper into your characters' minds and understand their motivations. You must always know what you are writing about.

THE DANGERS OF TOO MUCH ANALYSIS

At the same time you have to be careful of this sort of analysis. You can dignify anything if you try hard enough, and the tale of Slime and Elsie (the story of a woman of deep strength and a man of moral weakness) is already sounding like a textual analysis of *Macbeth*. In his book *The Way to Write for Television* Eric Paice points out that you can make *Little Red Riding Hood* mean anything from 'wolves should make sure there are no woodcutters around before they dress up in drag' to 'little girls should have their eyes tested before visiting their grandmothers'.

But a good play, whether it deals with contemporary social issues or not, should always operate on two levels: the story and the idea behind the story. Writing must go deep, and find, beneath the narrative, a thought that will illuminate our view of the world.

SUMMARY

- Be clear about the underlying theme of your play – the issues it raises, the emotions it explores. This will make it easier to plot your story, develop your characters, and reach an effective and powerful conclusion.

> A theme is an idea . . . about life and its meaning, about the human condition. It is the underlying truth signified by the film – universal, enduring, significant, expressive and eloquent. It springs from the writer's view of the way the world is and his sense of morality of the way the world should be.
>
> (William Miller, American writer and film maker)
>
> If you want to send a message, use Western Union.
>
> (Hollywood producer)

3

Style

WHAT TYPE OF PLAY ARE YOU WRITING?

You know your story, and your characters. You have considered the **theme** of your play – its message, the issues it deals with.

But what **style** should you write in? Will you write a straightforward, realistic, documentary-type of play, with the camera used as an unseen eye to record the scene? Or will you include elements of artifice – people speaking to camera, special effects, flash-backs, fantasy? As the play's narrator, will you allow viewers to know everything that is happening, or will you deliberately keep your audience in the dark about some aspects of the story to encourage their curiosity?

You might call a play 'a love story', but what kind of love story? You may decide to write a comedy, but is it:

- A social comedy, employing wit and irony?
- A farce?
- A black comedy?
- A savage satire?

Viewers will be confused (before them, of course, and more importantly, script readers will be confused) if a much-loved character suddenly develops cancer in the middle of a frothy farce, or if an exposé of homelessness in London is suddenly over-run with bikini-clad girls hiding in wardrobes.

You might argue that drama needs to tear itself free of conventions (Dennis Potter's drama did), but to break the conventions you need first to understand them and to have the ability to write within them. At the very least, you must be breaking them deliberately.

In this chapter we look at:

- plays that show the world as it is (called **narrative realism)**
- plays that utilize fantasy and the imagination (**non-realism**)
- ways to tell your story

- ways in which the camera can tell your story.

NARRATIVE REALISM

In narrative realism we are out there in real life, in the world of drizzly afternoons, Job Centres and supermarkets. The locations are real, the characters are credible, the stories believable. *Cathy Come Home* is the benchmark, a play that looked back to films like *Saturday Night and Sunday Morning* and *Room at the Top*. Critics say narrative realism is boring and pedestrian, doing something that ought to be done by the straightforward television documentary, and failing to use properly the possibilities of television. Nevertheless, this type of play has many defenders, and is the most accessible form of drama for the new writer. In recent years it has gained a new and controversial lease of life through the drama-documentary – fiction based on real events. Narrative realism plays are invariably filmed on location rather than in the studio.

In narrative realism you should maintain the following conventions:

- **Surface accuracy**. In simple terms this means that a fireman's uniform should be a real fireman's uniform. People who ask for drinks in pubs should have to pay for them – and if the price is mentioned it should be believable. The law of the land, as it exists in your script, should conform to the law as we understand it in the real world. If the main character in your crime thriller is a school headmistress, and you find that you want her to interrogate suspects (something that school headmistresses do not do), you must not let her do it without providing a logical, believable excuse.

- **Cause and effect**. At its simplest, if somebody is lying in the garden in a swimsuit we should expect it to be summer and the sun shining. If a woman punches a man violently in a restaurant, other diners should respond in a believable manner. (This will depend, of course, on where the event is taking place: Cheltenham diners might be expected to respond differently from diners in Rome.)

- **Psychological consistency**. If a character is sensible, they should remain sensible *unless their change in character is part of your story*. If a character suddenly stops being good-natured and becomes spiteful, viewers will try to find a reason, and puzzle over how it fits into the story you are telling.

- **Normal expectations of character and behaviour**. What is portrayed should conform to a common-sense view of what happens in the world. In some ways this is a dodgy rule, a great worry to the politically correct. It means that if the camera strays into a household of Asian immigrants we should expect to find a curry on the table. In the country mansion of Sir Roddy Forescue, Bart, we should expect to find roast beef. Reverse the menus without explanation, and viewers will be confused. They will fret over why Sir Roddy is munching curry and the immigrants passing the mustard.

  This is a perfectly valid rule, but it does inevitably reinforce stereotypes, and it can make scripts dull and predictable. The writer should try to present a view of the world that is credible but at the same time fresh and different, which is, of course, easier said than done.

NON-REALISTIC DRAMA

This can be simply heightened drama – the characters deliberately larger than life, as seen in many comedies – or it can move into fantasy and use the camera to show us images, ideas, thoughts that might be in the characters' heads. Some dramas combine realism with fantasy, notable examples being *Selling Hitler* and before that *Wingate* and David Rudkin's *Penda's Fen*. In *Trainspotting* the addict swims down the lavatory bowl seeking his lost drugs. Among modern television dramatists Dennis Potter was the most distinguished in carrying the torch for drama of the imagination.

The new writer is often tempted to write fantasy. It frees him from the tedious constraint of believable characterisation, logical plots and credible dialogue. But only the most skilled and confident – not to say established – writer can normally break conventions with impunity, and until he is in a position to explain his idea to Channel 4's Head of Drama over lunch, the new writer should stick to the grim business of devising stories that we can believe in.

On the other hand, a major new talent that is exciting and different and revolutionary in its use of the medium, must make – and break – the rules.

WAYS TO TELL YOUR STORY

The way you tell (**narrate**) your story depends on how best you think you can grip your audience and hold its interest.

The omniscient narrator

The narrator knows more than the characters, and lets viewers share the knowledge. In a crime story we see the murder committed. We know the identity of the murderer. We watch the detective stumbling – with many a false trail – towards the truth. This technique can give a valuable element of suspense (will the villain be caught or will the nice chap who has been framed get sent down for ten years by which time his poor widowed Mum will be dead?) but you lose the element of mystery.

The narrator as character

Sometimes the narrator knows only what the principal character knows. We unravel the mystery with the detective, sharing his or her thoughts. This is straight realism, the classic whodunnit.

The narrator as a tease

Sometimes the narrator pretends to know only what the principal characters know, but occasionally reveals other things to us. (Miss Brown stops sobbing and smiles bravely. Detective Inspector Boot takes back his hankie and leaves the room. Miss Brown's expression changes. She picks up the letter. She stares at it, her expression cold. She suddenly rips it into pieces. CUT to the next scene.) Here we cannot be certain that it was Miss Brown whodidit, but we know she is not what she seems – and we thus know more than the detective. This is a very dangerous technique, for if the camera can tell us a bit about what's happening, why can't it tell us everything?

The narrator in the dark

Sometimes the narrator knows less than the characters. Detective Inspector Boot says: 'So that is how he did it – no, don't ask me to tell you, not until my final experiment, but arrange for Madam de Courville and the ticket inspector to be entering this building at precisely 7pm.' This was the basis of the Sherlock Holmes stories, of course. In lesser hands it is a technique that can be infuriating. 'If Boot knows who did it why doesn't he tell us instead of being smug?'

The cheating narrator

The viewer will rapidly, if unconsciously, know which technique you are employing and will expect you to stick to it. If we are solving the crime in company with the detective and suddenly (tempted by the need for a dramatic moment) you show us, the viewers, something that the detective does not know, the play will be in danger of losing dramatic tension.

The real narrator

The real narrator, of course, knows everything. The real narrator (you the writer) has decided which dramatic technique to use.

WAYS THE CAMERA CAN NARRATE YOUR STORY

This is a topic that can get fairly esoteric, and is much debated by media course lecturers (is the camera being used in the mode of *histoire* or *discours*?). New writers should avoid getting bogged down in such questions.

At its simplest there are two basic narrative modes.

The impartial narrator

The camera has no viewpoint (although clearly somebody has selected the images and words). We see a succession of things happen as recorded by an impartial eye.

The active narrator

The camera overtly presents us with opinions on what is happening, or on the views that are being expressed (a pan along a wall of china ducks while a character says: 'I've always prided myself on my good taste'); or a character speaks to camera as Fielding did in *Tom Jones*; or glances to camera and winks as Francis Urquhart did in *House of Cards*.

SUMMARY

- Most writers use straightforward narrative realism but also employ the camera actively to point up mood, give pace, and emphasise characterisation. (See Chapter 6, Visual Interest.) This is an effective method and shows agents and editors that you can think visually and use the camera.

- Don't get bogged down worrying about who the narrator is. You will almost certainly get it right by instinct. Refer back to this chapter, though, if you get into trouble.

> To make a great movie, you need just three things: a great script, a great script, and a great script.
>
> (Alfred Hitchcock)

4

Structure

SIMPLER THAN IT LOOKS

Entire books are written about structure. There are those who believe in surface structure and deep structure, who can plot structure on a graph, who can tell you what to do between pages 1 and 5 and between pages 5 and 10 and so on. All this is useful and interesting for students of critical analysis but it can stifle the talents of a writer. Shakespeare, we can be confident, did not have little graphs of character development (set-up and focus point), story development (conflict and confrontation) and climax (moment of truth) on his desk when he penned *King Lear*.

If you take account of the following points you will get your structure right instinctively, without having your freedom to write as your imagination takes you unnecessarily constrained:

- the basic structure
- the opening
- classic hooks to keep viewers watching
- structuring for commercial breaks
- multi-strand structuring.

THE BASIC STRUCTURE

This is the broad shape of any play. Keep to it and you will not go far wrong.

1. **Situation**. You present us with a visual setting, the main characters, and the beginning of a story that interests us and makes us want to go on watching. This invariably involves conflict of some kind (see **conflict in drama**, page 40).

2. **Complication**. The situation you set up in the beginning needs to be complicated, false trails need to be laid, the aims and

ambitions of your characters frustrated. At the same time we must be clear about where we are heading, and our interest must not wane.

3. **Reversal**. If things went badly for your hero they should now change and start to go better. Conversely, if your hero has been doing well, things should now go badly (**retardation** of the story).

4. **Climax**. The central issue of your drama must come to a climax – the conflict come to a head. This can be done through dialogue or through action on the screen. As this is television, a visual climax is preferred. In series drama it is traditionally 'the car chase'. The car chase need not involve cars – it can be a gunman pursuing another through an empty warehouse, or anything else that involves action, movement and pace.

5. **Resolution**. Something must have changed. It may be a purely physical resolution (your hero and heroine united; your villain dragged off to gaol) or it may be an alteration in your characters' attitude to life, towards each other. Perhaps your **twist resolution** is that they are not changed at all. If aliens seize a gardener from his allotment and require him to undergo unbelievable terrors in order to save the galaxy – and the last thing we see is him back in his vegetable plot checking his potatoes and muttering 'The things you have to do in this life, I don't know...' – well, that is a resolution in itself.

Another way of putting it is to say that, however disguised, all plays need to have a beginning, a middle, and an end!

THE OPENING

The first 60 seconds are crucially important. The remote control unit has taught producers that viewers are fickle and disloyal. If they are not hooked in the first minute they are liable to press the button and 'zap' to another channel. One writer, chided by a script editor for having a slow opening, replied: 'I did it deliberately! It's to hook the people who have zapped over after the first minute on something else' – but this cunning excuse is unlikely to be accepted. A strong opening is particularly important for series dramas – *Casualty*, *London's Burning*, etc. – where episodes cost well over half a million pounds to make, and are designed to anchor the evening's audience and build audiences for future episodes.

The way to a good opening is to devise a good hook.

CLASSIC HOOKS TO KEEP VIEWERS WATCHING

Three classic hooks are:

- curiosity
- mystery
- suspense.

Curiosity

Curiosity is the basis of all story-telling. If humans were not intractably curious, if they did not by their very nature always want to know *what will happen next*, then novelists and dramatists would have a lean time of it.

> A woman rushes up to a man and says: 'Well, did you do it?' and he looks at her stony-faced, and then nods, and she says: 'O my God.' End of scene. Opening titles.

Hopefully, we are curious to know what the man has done. Murdered his wife? Had the cat put down? Left the bathroom tap running with disastrous consequences?

> A girl watches through the window as the postman approaches. She is clearly excited. The postman turns in at the gate, and the girl runs through to the hall as an expensive-looking white envelope falls to the mat. She picks it up and turns it over, longing to open it and yet frightened...

There is no mystery yet, because we have not been presented with anything mysterious or odd. But such is the human desire to know what other people are up to, and in particular the desire to see inside other people's letters, that even a mildly curious opening will help to keep viewers hooked.

Mystery

A more powerful hook is the use of mystery. Somebody does something strange, something we cannot account for. A dour, sinister man with a mean, cold face slips into a hotel room with a small plastic device that he furtively places behind a vase of flowers. What is it? A bomb? A microphone?

A man visits a private detective and asks that the Mother Superior of a nunnery should be followed night and day. He will not say why, or give an explanation, but he will pay treble the usual rate. What can she be up to?

Sherlock Holmes stories are built around mysteries; on television *The Avengers* always gave us an opening scene in which something totally odd and unaccountable happened. A huge number of plays and serials depend on the use of mystery to a greater or lesser extent – particularly in the first 60 seconds.

Suspense

Suspense is what keeps us on the edge of our seats. If mystery relies on puzzlement, and not knowing what is going on, suspense is when we know perfectly well what might happen, and are fearful in case it does.

> A shadow of a person against a wall in an alleyway, holding a knife. CUT TO: A girl walking along the dark, empty street towards the alley. CUT TO: A police car patrols in a well-lit street nearby. CUT TO: The shadow raises the knife as we hear the girl's footsteps approach. CUT TO: Interior of police car, the driver whistling softly as he turns the car into the dark empty street. CUT TO: The girl reaches the alleyway...

And so on. We are compelled to watch, even if we know that the girl cannot be killed because her engagement to the hero in the next episode is on the cover of *TV Times*.

STRUCTURING FOR COMMERCIAL BREAKS

Like the remote control zapper, commercial breaks give viewers the opportunity to switch to another channel. When structuring a serial or series episode it is vital to lead up to a cliff-hanger before each break. It can involve curiosity, mystery, or suspense – the important thing is that it must make us want to go on watching. When you submit a synopsis or storyline of an episode, the script editor will be looking to see if you have strong commercial breaks.

The one thing you must not do is cheat the viewer. If the dour sinister man with a mean, cold face has slipped furtively into the hotel room, and we have heard edgy ominous music as he carefully placed the plastic device behind the vase of flowers, it is cheating to come back after the commercial break to discover that he is a hotel porter putting air ionisers into the guest rooms.

MULTI-STRAND STRUCTURING

Many plays – and particularly series dramas – have more than one plot. Many have two separate plots and also a comic **sub-plot**. Skilled and experienced writers know how to keep different stories bubbling, but the following tips might be helpful for new writers.

Do not attempt to introduce both stories at once

When you open your play you have to impart a lot of information to the viewers very quickly:

- the visual scene
- the initial characters, their names, backgrounds, the role they have to play
- the initial story
- the 'hook' that will keep people watching.

And you have to do all this in a taut, dramatic and interesting way.

It is hard enough to do this with one major story without confusing the viewer with *two* sets of information.

It makes sense to spend the first half-dozen scenes setting up the first story, take it to a point where it can conveniently rest for a moment (preferably with a good 'hook' to keep people interested), and then turn to story number two.

Try to devise stories that are quite different from each other

This helps with **pace**. A story that needs a lot of explaining, a lot of dialogue, a lot of concentration on what is said, needs to be contrasted with a story that is basically simple and has action.

In the *Boon* episode, *Peacemaker*, examined in Chapter 6, page 51, there are three stories:

1. A pop star due to make his comeback on the Birmingham music scene goes missing. Boon and Margaret have to track him down. This is basically comedy-drama. It is highly visual involving

stake-outs and chases through sleazy pubs.

2. A woman wants her husband followed to get proof that he is cheating with his alimony payments. This story is more serious, it is about the consequences of divorce, it has twists as our sympathies are engaged first with one side and then with the other.

3. A comedy sub-story involves Harry entertaining a delegation of Dutch machine tool manufacturers in the Plaza Suite.

In *Peacemaker* the writers are careful to make sure that a comedy-drama sequence from story one is followed by a quieter and more down-to-earth scene from story two; and a scene which imparts a lot of information through dialogue is followed by a scene which is visual.

SUMMARY

- In broad terms the first part of your script (25 per cent) should set up the situation: the second part (50 per cent) should complicate or deepen it; the third part (25 per cent) should resolve it. Ignore these proportions, however, if they do not fit your particular story.
- Hook the reader on page one by creating curiosity, mystery or suspense.
- Always have one of these hooks – curiosity, mystery, suspense – operating on some sort of level.
- If you are running two stories, allow the first to be established before introducing the second.
- Do not overwhelm viewers with verbal information, particularly in the beginning.

> A good *Boon* episode? – the girl shows her tits and you end up with a car chase.
>
> (Former producer, Central TV's *Boon*)

5

Plotting

HOW DO YOU MAKE THE PLOT INTERESTING?

You have a story, you have worked out a broad structure, now take a look at how you can write the script in an interesting way. This chapter deals with the following:

- the importance of conflict
- decision-making by principal characters
- consequence of action – cause and effect
- creating sympathy
- plots to avoid.

CONFLICT IN DRAMA

All drama depends on conflict. That is not the same as saying that drama depends on people shouting at each other. Generally speaking, people shouting at each other should be avoided – most people have enough argument in their lives without watching other people bawling their heads off. At its most basic, conflict means that Character A wants something to happen, and Character B wants something different to happen.

This might mean anything from: A murderer wants to escape – a detective wants to arrest him. A schoolmaster wants promotion – another wants to sabotage him. A girl wants a bloke – another girl wants him as well. A girl wants a bloke – another bloke wants the girl. A husband wants bacon for breakfast – his wife wants him to have high-fibre muesli.

What does conflict mean?

It can mean:

- a problem to be solved
- an obstacle to be overcome

- a threat to be handled
- a decision to be made
- a challenge to be met.

Conflict is not the same as aggression. You could write a 50-minute play based on the conflict between a child who wants a kitten, and her family who don't. You could show her manipulations, her relentless purchase of kitten books, her feverish illness caused by not having a kitten, her letters to Father Christmas, finally her finding (or buying) a kitten and bringing it home and hiding it... and the entire play could be gentle and humorous and non-aggressive.

> There is only one plot in TV drama. There's a guy in Zanzibar with a cork up his arse. The only guy in the world who can get it out lives in Newark, New Jersey. We spend the next 50 minutes watching the second guy fighting overwhelming odds to reach the first guy before he dies of toxic poisoning.
>
> (US film distributor)

What does conflict include?

It can include the following:

Man versus elements

Can the mountaineers reach the top of Everest before the storm descends? Will superb seamanship bring the yacht with a hole in it safe to harbour? Can the cork-extracting man from New Jersey fight his way on foot through the Zanzibar jungle?

Man versus time

Can the cork-extracting man from New Jersey fight his way through the Zanzibar jungle in time? Can the rescue squad find the boy lost in the potholes before he dies of hunger? Can the hero struggling on foot through the blizzard (man versus elements) reach the girl in the wooden shack before the rapist arrives in his snowmobile?

Man versus himself

Can Sir Thomas More reconcile his conscience to swearing allegiance to Henry VIII as head of the Church? Can the Old Labour MP accept the British Telecom shares left to him by his aunty? Can the student who cheated at her exam accept the prize scholarship, knowing that she is depriving a fellow-student who is desperately hard-up? Can the newly divorced man conquer his overwhelming depression?

THE IMPORTANCE OF DECISION-MAKING

Dramatic tension is held if the story develops through decisions made by the main characters. It is not held if the story develops through coincidence and arbitrary accidents. When that happens it ceases to be a story and becomes a succession of incidents.

The viewers need to see a central character faced with a problem. They need to see the options available. They need to see a decision taken – and then to see the result. If a character has to achieve a goal you should put as many obstacles as possible in his path, force him to take as many decisions as possible, and then show how he copes.

Arbitrary accidents can form obstacles – the cork-extractor man from New Jersey might be speeding across Africa in a train that breaks down. But this is a device to offer a new decision to be taken: does he wait for the train to be mended or hitch a ride on a poorly-looking camel owned by a one-eyed bandit with a sharp knife? If he goes on the camel will it collapse or will the bandit kill him?

It is important that decisions should be left to your central characters. In this case the bandit must either be innocent of evil intent, or waiting to pounce. It will almost certainly not work if you switch the focus, and have the bandit making a decision: do I kill this cork-extractor man or not? If I do will I escape with his money or get caught?

It will also be profoundly unsatisfactory if the man from New Jersey fails to reach the man with the corked arse because he catches a cold and has to go to bed, where a snake that we knew nothing about bites him and he dies.

CONSEQUENCES OF ACTION: CAUSE AND EFFECT

> The King died and then the Queen died. That is a story. The King died and then the Queen died of *grief*. That is a plot.
>
> (E. M. Forster, *Aspects of the Novel*)

A plot is basically the relationship of cause and effect. Something happens, and as a result something else happens. You set up a uation and then see how your characters react to it. Based on what do, a new situation is created, and so the story moves on...

CREATING SYMPATHY

It is useful to have at least *one* sympathetic character and to introduce him at an early stage. Viewers like to know who to identify with, they like to know who they should be cheering for. You can, of course, show a pleasant character and later reveal a vicious side to his nature – and you can have a vile person who turns out to have all kinds of redeeming features. But at the beginning of a play we need to establish something, or somebody, that viewers can *care about*.

PLOTS TO AVOID

The idiot plot

Script editors hate plots which can only work if basically intelligent characters behave in a totally stupid way. *Dr Who* was always a terrible culprit here – the Doctor and his Assistant would be clinging to each other in some noisome underground cave system, we would all *know* they ought to stay together, but sure enough the Doctor would say: 'I'll be back in a minute', and wander off on his own, leaving his assistant to be captured and held prisoner for the next four episodes. In *Dr Who* this was expected, it was part of the formula, but it is basically very lazy plotting.

Story development should stem from character. You should never force characters unnaturally to obey your plot.

Scenes that go nowhere

Every scene should move the story on. It should advance the plot or illuminate the characters – preferably both. Beware of scenes that repeat the plot but in a slightly different way. If you write a scene, and then find you can cut it out of your script without losing anything relevant to the story, then cut it.

Plots that lose tension

We must always want to know what is going to happen next. If a scene satisfies curiosity roused in previous scenes, it should also arouse curiosity about events in the future. Plots often lose tension because:

- you have resolved conflict elements too soon, and there is nothing left for us to anticipate
- your plot has become bogged down in explanations of past

events; viewers are rarely kept on the edge of their seats by verbal explanations of what has gone before

- it was a boring idea to start with.

SUMMARY

- The 'plot' is the order of events in which you choose to tell the 'story'.
- All drama depends on conflict – but conflict does not have to mean aggression.
- Do not devise plots that can only work if your characters are stupid. Never force characters unnaturally to obey your plot.
- Do not let your plot get bogged down in verbal explanations of previous scenes.

> The 'story' is what actually happens, the material of the tale, and the 'plot' is the way a narrative is realised.
> (Patricia Holland, *The Television Handbook*)

6

Visual Interest

You have come up with a brilliant idea, and you have worked out a plot showing how the story will develop. The third thing you need to be able to do is to *tell your story in an interesting way.*

This chapter will look at:

- visual interest on screen
- using pictures instead of words
- ways to maintain dramatic tension
- opening scenes of a *Boon* episode.

HOW TO INCREASE VISUAL INTEREST

Watch any popular drama series on ITV and note how short most scenes are, how quickly we move about, and how few scenes take place in visually boring places like offices or sitting rooms (in other words locations reminiscent of studio plays). In *Peacemaker*, the *Boon* episode looked at in this chapter, there are only three scenes set in the detective agency's office. When a director comes across a wordy, static indoor scene with two people talking to each other, his first instinct is to move the scene to somewhere else: somewhere visually interesting. The longer and more wordy (or delicate and sensitive as you the writer might put it) the scene, the more he will want to break it up with movement, and before you know it your characters will be playing squash or practising on the high trapeze. Even if restrained from his wilder notions, the director would rather have characters walking sedately along a river bank than sitting on opposite sides of a table. This gives him **variety of shots** and allows him to punctuate the dramatic content of the scene with **movement**.

You give the director this:

INT. KITCHEN. DAY.

MARY AND JOHN ARE STILL SITTING AT THE KITCHEN

TABLE. HIS HEAD IS SLUMPED.

MARY: John? If you've got something to say then I'd rather you said it.

JOHN LOOKS UP

JOHN: OK. All right. I've been having an affair with Tracy from the catfood factory.

MARY TURNS AWAY SHARPLY. JOHN PAUSES, SHATTERED FOR A MOMENT HAVING FINALLY BROUGHT HIMSELF TO TELL HER. THEN HE CONTINUES WITH NEW CONFIDENCE:

We love each other and I want a divorce. I want children and you can't give me children. I know it's not your fault, I know that you desperately want children yourself, but there's no reason for us both to suffer –

MARY: Stop it, stop it, stop it!

And the director gives you back this:

EXT. RIVERBANK. DAY

MARY AND JOHN WALK ON PAST THE WEIR, UNDER THE FALLING LEAVES OF AUTUMN. THEY ARE STILL SILENT WITH MISERY. MARY STOPS AND THROWS BREAD TO A SWAN AND HER CYGNETS.

MARY: John? (HE DOES NOT RESPOND) If you've got something to say then I'd rather you said it.

JOHN: OK. All right. I've been having an affair with Tracy from the catfood factory.

MARY FREEZES. THE MOTHER SWAN AND HER CYGNETS ARE EATING THE BREAD. JOHN PAUSES, SHATTERED FOR A MOMENT HAVING FINALLY BROUGHT HIMSELF TO TELL HER. THEN HE CONTINUES WITH NEW CONFIDENCE. WE WATCH THE

SWAN AND HER CYGNETS FROM MARY'S POV:

JOHN: (OOV) We love each other and I want a divorce. I want children, and you can't give me children. I know it's not your fault, I know that you desperately want children yourself, but there's no reason for us both to suffer –

CUT SHARPLY BACK TO MARY WHO TURNS

MARY: Stop it, stop it, stop it!

THE SWAN FLAPS HER WINGS IN ALARM AND HER CYGNETS SCATTER.

The second version allows the story to progress visually (in this scene we are at the weir, in a previous scene we would have been on another part of the river bank); allows us to have a decent dramatic pause for John and still have something to look at; gives us a nice bit of symbolism looking at a Mum and her little ones while John cruelly rambles on about childlessness; and the ominous rumble of the weir in the background offers a hint that Mary might either drown herself or, preferably, drown John.

USING PICTURES INSTEAD OF WORDS

Before writing a word of dialogue, always ask yourself whether any dialogue is necessary at all.

(Malcolm Hulke, writer)

Picture the following scene:

A group round a coffin in a country graveyard. The vicar intoning from the *Book of Common Prayer*. We see the Range Rovers and the BMWs parked on the verges of the country lane, the rooks cawing round their nests in the dead elm trees. The camera PANS along thoughtful, sober faces, until it finds JASPER, who is surreptitiously smiling behind his asthma inhaler.

Cut to DOLORES, who shoots him a glance of pure hate.

CUT TO: Shovels of earth fall on the coffin. The rooks caw, the vicar intones, and we suddenly become aware of heavy laboured breathing... the breathing of somebody struggling for life.

CUT TO: The rooks wheel round the elms.

CUT TO: JASPER begins to turn blue, his breath wheezing. Somebody screams. JASPER falls into the open grave.

CUT TO: DOLORES turns away. Her hand lightly checks the side pocket of her Burberry, to make sure the zip is fastened. She strolls towards the church gate.

We don't need a competition to see how pictures here can substitute for words in setting the scene (England, C of E, middle-class, rural, springtime because the rooks are nesting, a burial) and also in telling the story (Jasper murdered by Dolores who has the asthma inhaler poison in her Burberry pocket) – and all without a word of dialogue apart from the words of Archbishop Cranmer, who is out of copyright anyway.

Looking at the scenes from *Peacemaker* on pages 51–58 you will see how the scenes with dialogue are punctuated by scenes which move the story along purely with the use of pictures.

DRAMATIC TENSION

You must always have something on screen that holds the interest of the viewer. It might be one of the following:

- **A development of the plot** – our attention is held because we have become involved in the characters and the story, and we want to know what will happen next.
- **Emotion** – happiness, shock, tears. It is distressing but true that people are fascinated by other people's emotional reactions.
- **Humour** – an interlude involving a humorous theme might not move the plot forward or reveal anything new, but providing we laugh all can be forgiven. In *Peacemaker* we have two pop concert promoters who have 'lost' their star – and Boon is trying to find him. We need to cut back to the promoters now and again, simply so that we will not forget their existence. In plot terms the obvious thing would be to show them sitting in their sordid office, waiting – or on the phone to our detectives demanding to know what was happening. Instead the writers run a small sub-theme in which the promoters' sidekick tries to prove his cleverness by suggesting alternative stars. In one scene he is

inspired to utter the words 'Gary Glitter', and the promoter opens the window and howls like a soul in torture; in another he modestly suggests his younger brother, and the promoter snarls: 'I've billed this as a comeback. How can your brother come back? He hasn't been anywhere.'

- **Visual interest** – by providing movement, rapid cuts from location to location, interesting locations, people running, vehicles moving at speed, what we see on the screen can help sustain dramatic tension.

Things that lose dramatic tension

- Scenes or fragments of dialogue that do not go anywhere, and do not relate to the story or plot.

- Scenes that repeat themselves and fail to move the story on.

- Characters that fail to react in a logical manner. To a considerable extent viewers look to the reactions of characters in a play in order to work out their own reactions. If a woman hits a man in a restaurant and nobody pays any attention, and the man carries on eating his food, then there will be no dramatic tension. But if the entire restaurant falls silent, and the man stares in cold fury and the woman begins to shake – then there is dramatic tension.

A LOOK AT THE OPENING OF A *BOON* EPISODE

We've looked at some elements that go into telling a story on television. Now take a look at a professional script.

Boon was a Central Television drama series about a private detective, Ken Boon, played by Michael Elphick. It was comedy-drama, but occasionally with a hard edge. Six series were made and the programme moved locations during each series. An outstanding episode was *Peacemaker* written by Diane Culverhouse and Julian Spilsbury for Series Three.

At the time Ken Boon and Margaret Daley were partners in a small Birmingham private detective agency. The agency's office was at the back of the Plaza Suite – a run-down function venue owned by Ken's old friend Harry.

The main story in *Peacemaker* opens with the following situation:

A Midland pop star, Bograt, is due to attend a 'comeback' recording session in Birmingham. He loses his nerve and disappears. The promoters hire Boon and Margaret to track him down.

How would you write the first scene, explaining the situation?

The following openings were suggested by students at a television drama seminar.

> *Suggestion one*
> Boon's office. CLOSE UP of a newspaper with a photograph of Bograt and headline 'Comeback for Brum pop star'. PULL BACK to show promoter asking Boon and Margaret to take on the case.

The use of the newspaper picture is good, but otherwise this is a very boring, non-visual opening that does little to whet our curiosity and depends on our absorbing a lot of information through dialogue rather than pictures.

> *Suggestion two*
> Bograt arrives at Birmingham railway station, or airport, and is surrounded by fans. As he leaves the station he is pounced on and pushed into a car that disappears at speed.

Nice and visual and it ought to arouse our curiosity – but Bograt is supposed to disappear in panic, not be kidnapped. All right, he could have set up the kidnap himself, but why come back to Birmingham at all in that case? Is he, perhaps, going into hiding just to seek publicity?

Trying to find a logical motivation for the visually-interesting kidnap is changing the entire storyline – and we are only in scene one!

This opening adds a further complication: the disappearance is now public knowledge, and one area of dramatic tension – only a small group of people aware that he has disappeared – has been lost to us.

> *Suggestion three*
> Bograt on stage at a comeback concert. It's a huge success/ miserable failure. Backstage afterwards the promoter goes to Bograt's dressing room and finds it empty... and the window open.

This is good and visual. The concert must, presumably, be a success or the promoter is not going to care whether Bograt disappears or not. But if it is a success, then Bograt *has already made his comeback* – and to some extent at least the story is over. Also, if it is a success, why has he done a bunk?

On a practical level, it is hugely expensive to hire a theatre, put in lighting, stage a pop concert, and fill the theatre with people just to get 30 seconds of material.

Here is how the writers of *Peacemaker* tackled the opening, and also how they introduced the other stories in the episode.

1. EXT. BIRMINGHAM STREET. NIGHT.
A LARGE HOTEL, THERE IS LOUD, HEAVY METAL MUSIC FROM AN UPPER FLOOR WINDOW. THE MUSIC STOPS ABRUPTLY. THERE IS SHOUTING. A WINDOW BREAKS. A BLACK LEATHERY FIGURE (BOGRAT) EMERGES AND RACES DOWN A FIRE ESCAPE.

WE SEE HIS FACE BRIEFLY BEFORE HE LOPES OFF INTO THE NIGHT.

2. INT. MARGARET'S BEDROOM. NIGHT.
MARGARET IN BED ASLEEP IS WOKEN BY THE PHONE RINGING. SHE PICKS UP THE RECEIVER, GRUMPILY LOOKING AT THE CLOCK.

MARGARET: Hello?... Speaking... (WINCES) What, now? Yes, I know it.... I'll be right round. (SLIGHTLY INCREDULOUS) What did you say his name was?

3. INT. HOTEL LUXURY SUITE. NIGHT.
PROMOTIONAL MATERIAL ADVERTISES THE 'BOGRAT AND THE NEKROS' COMEBACK ALBUM. BOGRAT FEATURES PROMINENTLY. THE ROOM IS A SCENE OF DEVASTATION. THE MINI FRIDGE IS DRY, THE DOOR HANGS OFF. BOTTLES, CANS, CIGARETTE ENDS LITTER EVERY SURFACE. BOGRAT'S MANAGER LENNY BRIGHT IS STUMPING ANGRILY ROUND THE ROOM. GEOFF, HIS GOPHER, IS JUST FINISHING THE CALL TO MARGARET. A GIRL, NIKKI, IS SPACED OUT AND SOBBING. THE MEN IGNORE HER.

GEOFF: She's coming straight over.

LENNY: Nice work, Geoff!

GEOFF: I only turned my back for five minutes!

LENNY: He didn't need five minutes. (Thinks) Were you with a bird?

GEOFF: (FOLLOWING HIM AROUND THE ROOM) It was a call of nature. The en suite was full.

LENNY: (PEERS INTO BATHROOM) Good grief. (TURNS AWAY) It still is.

THE HOTEL MANAGER ENTERS AND LOOKS ROUND IN HORROR AT THE DEVASTATION.

MANAGER: Oh my god!

LENNY: (TO GEOFF) Pay the man.

GEOFF GOES OVER DRAGGING OUT HIS WALLET

4. EXT. BIRMINGHAM STREET. NIGHT
A POLICE CAR, SIREN GOING, PULLS UP AT A PUNCH-UP OUTSIDE A SEEDY NIGHT CLUB. THE BLACK LEATHERY FIGURE OF BOGRAT SURVEYS THE SCENE WITH EVIDENT SATISFACTION, THEN TURNS AND WALKS AWAY.

HE LOOKS ROUND HIM AT THE TATTY STREETS, THEN PUNCHES THE AIR AND JUMPS FOR JOY. HE IS HOME, AND HE IS FREE.

5. INT. HOTEL LOBBY. NIGHT
MARGARET CROSSES FOYER AND ENTERS LIFT.

6. INT. HOTEL SUITE. OUTER ROOM. NIGHT
GEOFF IS BUYING OFF THE HOTEL MANAGER. THERE IS A PILE OF £20 NOTES BETWEEN THEM TO WHICH GEOFF KEEPS ADDING. BEHIND THEM SITS NIKKI, STILL SOBBING AND IGNORED.

MANAGER: Carpets. Duvets...

MARGARET ENTERS

MARGARET: Mr Bright?

GEOFF: Just follow the wreckage. (TO MANAGER) Where were we?

MARGARET GOES THROUGH TO THE INNER ROOM.

MANAGER: Carpets.

GEOFF: Two-hundred-and-fifty.

NIKKI: I'm going to be sick!

MANAGER: No you don't!

HE DIVES TOWARDS HER. GEOFF SLIPS A COUPLE OF NOTES BACK OFF THE PILE.

7. INT. HOTEL LUXURY SUITE. INNER ROOM. NIGHT

LENNY: Lenny Bright. 'Bright Ideas'.

MARGARET: I understand you're missing a lead singer.

LENNY: (GESTURES TO A POSTER) You remember the Nekros?

MARGARET: (TACTFUL) Perhaps you'd refresh my memory.

LENNY: Split up five years ago, I've got them back together. Or at least, I had got them back together.

MARGARET: Well done.

LENNY: We're doing a come-back album, but it won't be worth a fart in a thunderstorm without *him*.

MARGARET: Bograt?

LENNY: You see? You do remember! That's what makes him special. I found him in Calais.

MARGARET: Calais?

LENNY: (NODS) It'll be engraved on my heart too.

MARGARET: What was he doing in Calais?

LENNY: On his way to Monte Carlo. He'd been on his way to Monte Carlo for five years. It was as far as he got.

MARGARET: And now he's gone again?

LENNY: Has a bust up with his girlfriend and (POINTS TO WINDOW) vroom!

MARGARET: Couldn't he use a door like anyone else?

LENNY: He isn't like anyone else!

MARGARET: And you want me to find him?

LENNY: And fast! I've got a studio, session artists, a producer, all standing idle.

MARGARET: (LOOKS AT POSTER) Is this fairly recent?

LENNY: We've a video in the office that's better.

MARGARET: I'll send somebody round for it. (LOOKS AT NIKKI, WHO IS NOW BEING TENDED BY GEOFF) I take it that's the girlfriend?

LENNY: (NODS) How is she, Geoff?

GEOFF: (WAVES A HAND IN FRONT OF HER FACE) Nikki? (NO RESPONSE) The lights are on but there's no one in.

MARGARET: I'll talk to her in the morning. Mr Bright, this won't be easy. If somebody really wants to hide –

LENNY: I want you on this full time. Usual rates. Two hundred quid bonus if you get him within forty-eight hours.

MARGARET: But he could be out of the country by morning.

LENNY SHAKES HIS HEAD. HE DRAWS HER TO THE WINDOW. HE TURNS OFF THE LIGHT. THEY LOOK OUT OVER BIRMINGHAM AT NIGHT, AND WE LOOK WITH THEM.
LENNY'S VOICE CHOKES WITH EMOTION.

LENNY: That's what brought him back. That city crouched down there like a beast. Those streets, those subways, they gave him everything. Life, art, inspiration. This is his city. Bograt's town.

8. INT. PLAZA SUITE. DAY
HARRY IS IN HIS BEST SUIT. HIS MINIONS ARE PREPARING A PROMOTION FOR A DUTCH MACHINE-TOOL COMPANY. THERE ARE LITTLE DUTCH FLAGS, BUNCHES OF PLASTIC TULIPS, AND A DUTCH-STYLE BUFFET BEING LAID OUT BY LINDA. HARRY CROSSES TO HER, HOLDING A LITTLE DUTCH PHRASE BOOK.

HARRY: Linda, what do you think 'Ik geloof dat ik voed-selvergiftiging hab' means?

LINDA: How about 'Go away and let me finish this buffet in peace?'

HARRY: (LAUGHS) Very close! Actually it's 'I think I've got food poisoning.'

HARRY SAMPLES SOMETHING FROM A PLATE. LINDA SNATCHES IT AWAY.

LINDA: Actually that pumpernickel's in short supply, Mr Crawford.

HARRY: (PULLS FACE) I'm glad to hear it. (CALLS) Can you put the music on now?

MARGARET HAS WALKED IN. HARRY APPROACHES HER. SHE LOOKS TIRED.

HARRY: Morning Margaret. Or should I say 'Goede Morgen'?

MARGARET: Very good. Who's coming, Queen Beatrix?

HARRY: A big machine-tool company from Utrecht, here for the week. Quite a coup, actually.

MARGARET: You've certainly done them proud. All you need now is –

THE MUSIC STARTS UP. IT IS MAX BYGRAVES SINGING 'TULIPS FROM AMSTERDAM'.

MARGARET: (FINISHES SENTENCE) Max Bygraves singing 'Tulips from Amsterdam'.

HARRY WINKS AT HER. HE IS ONE UP.

9. INT. BDI OFFICE. PLAZA SUITE. DAY
KEN IS TALKING TO A NERVOUS YOUNG WOMAN, WE CAN STILL HEAR THE MUSIC AND SO CAN THEY. THE WOMAN TURNS TO LOOK IN THE DIRECTION OF THE NOISE.

ELAINE: (SMILES SADLY) We went there on our honeymoon.

KEN: (SMILES COMFORTINGLY, REFERS TO HIS NOTES). This business 'Luxor Bathroom Fittings'. Does he own it?

ELAINE: No. He's the branch manager.

KEN: Still, he's doing all right?

ELAINE: Doing very well by all accounts. (SIGHS) I sound like a money-grabbing bitch, don't I?

KEN: Course not. The court awarded you maintenance.

MARGARET ENTERS

MARGARET: Morning Ken, we've got the most amazing... oh, I beg your pardon.

KEN: Mrs Bache, this is my partner, Margaret Daley.

ELAINE: How do you do.

MARGARET: Hello. I'll leave you to it.
SHE COLLECTS UP HER POST, SMILES AND EXITS.

ELAINE: (ON VERGE OF TEARS) I've got bills to pay. And if he's earning more than he says he's earning, well it's not fair, is it?

KEN: You're sure that's what he's doing?

ELAINE: Well I can't afford to go gadding round town all the time.

KEN: And he can?

ELAINE: That's what I've heard.
KEN: Women?

ELAINE: I don't know. Friends don't like to tell you about other women, do they?

KEN: No, still, it's possible. (LOOKS AT PHOTOGRAPH) He's not a bad-looking bloke, is he?

ELAINE: Appearances can be very deceptive. He's a bastard, Mr Boon. A real bastard.

How does the opening of *Peacemaker* work?

Scene One
The opening is visual and fast moving, from the window smashing to the darkened figure racing down the fire escape. The fire escape sequence also allows time for the **opening titles.**

Scene Two
In one line we establish that the Boon agency is being involved and that the matter is urgent. Curiosity is roused by the incredulous: 'What did you say his name was?'

Scene Three
In only eight lines of dialogue we are given two points of conflict and a second story strand is established:

- Lenny blames Geoff for losing Bograt, Geoff is resentful
- the hotel manager is horrified by the wreckage: Geoff is told to sort him out.

Scene Four
Bograt, enjoying his freedom. It is totally visual but tells us a lot about his character and the situation he is in.

Scene Five
Again is totally visual, showing Margaret arriving at the hotel.

Scene Six and Scene Seven
The basic situation is explained to Margaret – but note how we have the secondary story of Geoff and the hotel manager to divert us – the manager demanding heavy payment, Geoff doling the money out, Nikki the girlfriend almost being sick, Geoff pinching back some money, Nikki collapsing in a drunken stupor.

Note how future development is set up: Margaret asks if a poster is recent, Lenny says he has a video, Margaret says she'll send somebody round for it.

Scene Eight
A very visual scene with Dutch flags, tulips and buffet in the Plaza Suite sets up the comic subplot and brings Margaret in.

Scene Nine
The mood changes entirely as the second main story is set up. The music 'Tulips from Amsterdam' links the two scenes – but now has sad connotations. This scene has to give solid information, but note how it is given to us through natural dialogue – through the nervousness and distress of Elaine – and how the scene ends with an ominous warning for the future: 'He's a bastard, Mr Boon, a real bastard'. Also note that although the scene is only two pages long, it has been broken up by the entry of Margaret.

All three stories have now been introduced – and we have learned as much through the eye of the camera as through dialogue.

SUMMARY

- Avoid long scenes full of verbal explanation.
- Avoid long indoor scenes set in one room.
- Whenever possible use pictures rather than words to tell your story.
- Moving quickly between short scenes will increase pace and maintain tension.

7

Dialogue

THE THREE FUNCTIONS OF DIALOGUE

Dialogue is traditionally said to have three functions.

1. **To advance the story**. Just as each scene in a play should move the story forward, so each line of dialogue – or sequence of lines – should also move the plot onwards. Dialogue which repeats itself, or tells us things we know already, or gets bogged down in side issues, will destroy the dramatic tension of the scene.

2. **To reveal character**. A good line not only moves the story forward, it also reveals some facet, however minor, of the speaker's personality. See how Anna's character emerges from the two speeches quoted on page 61.

3. **To give us information**. Good dialogue gives us a mass of information – but without us realising it. If you look at the opening of the *Boon* episode on page 51 you will see how few words have actually been used to set up three stories and introduce half a dozen characters.

HOW TO CREATE CHARACTER THROUGH DIALOGUE

Everyone speaks differently, uses different vocabulary, different speech patterns. The characters in your play should be identifiable by their speech and the expressions they use. A common piece of advice is: after you have written a page of dialogue put a ruler over the names of the characters and then see if you can identify the speakers from their words alone.

Intelligence, class, education, geographical background – all these things contribute to the way people speak. It is a useful dramatic device to give characters expression of their own: the most famous perhaps being Walter Gabriel's 'Me old pal me old beauty' in *The*

Archers, or references to 'She who must be obeyed' in *Rumpole*. Read *The Importance of Being Earnest* and see that for all Wilde's stylisation, the languid speech patterns of Lady Bracknell contrast with the down-to-earth speech of Gwendoline.

COLOUR AND TEXTURE

> The barge she sat in, like a burnish'd throne,
> Burn'd on the water; the poop was beaten gold,
> Purple the sails, and so perfumed, that
> The winds were love-sick with them, the oars were silver
> Which to the tune of flutes kept stroke, and made
> The water which they beat to follow faster,
> As amorous of their strokes.
>
> (Shakespeare, *Anthony and Cleopatra*)

Most television dialogue imitates documentary realism, and you are not expected to be overly lyrical in your average *Casualty* or *Eastenders*. But dialogue needs colour and texture. However naturalistic on the surface, it needs to paint pictures with words. In the script layout example on page 147 a girl desperately in love with a CND supporter tells us that she has been on a protest march. In terms of plot all she needs to say is: 'I went on a march'. But the writer tells us much more than that:

> ANNA... I went on a march – my red slingbacks with four-inch heels all though London, past all the shops and I didn't go in, not even down Sloane Street.

In a single line we are given a picture of Anna on her march, tottering along in red slingbacks with her eyes on the shop windows rather than the protest banners. In an earlier scene in the play Anna admits that she is not actually interested in CND. Her friend Daisy says: 'I'm not convinced your heart's in it' and the simple, flat answer would be: 'No, you're right, it isn't.' In the script, though, we get:

> ANNA: Of course it isn't – the whole thing's totally tedious. I'm not interested in aeroplanes and fighting and wars – that's boy's stuff. American bases and NATO bases and all the bombs have got daft names and numbers. Why hasn't Simon noticed me?

Quality of dialogue, expressed through vocabulary and images, is what stamps your own signature on a script. If you gave Alan Bennett, Simon Gray and David Edgar an identical subject on which to write, they would all produce excellent, well-structured, well-characterised plays – but each would be totally different. This would be caused largely by their different views of life, but we would be made most aware of it through each writer's distinctive dialogue.

ECONOMY WITH WORDS

When Oscar Wilde said he had spent all morning deciding to put a comma in a sentence, and all afternoon deciding to take it out, he was probably telling no more than the truth.

In a film or television script every word should count. Every word should have its purpose. Once you have written a scene, go back through it and see how many lines you can lose, how many words you can strike out without losing either plot, atmosphere, or characterisation. You must be your own first script editor – and the more ruthless you are the better.

Dramatic dialogue is superficially naturalistic, but in fact is highly artificial. In real life people 'um' and they 'ah', they don't finish their sentences, they employ a surprisingly limited vocabulary, and they generally use ten words where one will do.

The art of television dialogue is to write something that *looks* naturalistic, but in which every word has a place and a purpose.

> Most people said how vivid and realistic the Liverpool dialogue was in *No Trains to Lime Street*. In fact, no one in Liverpool ever spoke as I make them speak in the play.
>
> (Alun Owen)

SUBTEXT

Subtext sounds a bit technical and advanced – it's the sort of word (the favourite is **genre**) that script editors like to use. Really it is very simple. The subtext is the meaning that is being conveyed, when the meaning is different from the words actually spoken.

When the lecher sidles up to the girl on a dusky summer's evening and murmurs: 'Why don't we go into the garden and look at the Old English roses?' and she looks him coolly up and down before smiling discretely and saying: 'Yes, why not?' – we know full well that they are not anticipating a chat about horticulture and ways to combat greenfly.

And when another girl hears the conversation and watches them leave and turns indignantly to another person and says: 'My god, did you see that? What an oily bastard – and what a tart she is!', we know that elements of personal jealousy are bubbling beneath the surface.

The commonly quoted example of subtext through pictures is the scene in the film *Tom Jones* where Tom and Mrs Waters eat a meal with their fingers in an outrageously seductive manner. The pictures show them devouring their food; the subtext tells us that they are devouring each other.

THE THROUGH LINE

The first thing an actor does when he opens a script is to see how big his part is. The next thing he looks for is a 'through line' for his character.

He is looking for a logical progress of thoughts and ideas. He can only memorise his lines if one thought leads to another thought, one exchange of dialogue leads, logically, to another. Actors find lines difficult to learn if the thoughts and expressions are illogical or repetitive.

'BAD LANGUAGE'

Language is extraordinarily powerful; much more powerful than pictures. A BBC survey in 1987 showed that strong disapproval of bad language exceeded strong disapproval of sex on television by a margin of three to one. Television transmits into people's homes, where three generations, from children to grandparents, might be watching at the same time. Television companies therefore have to be careful about the language they use.

There is an evening watershed at nine o'clock. Before then certain words cannot – or should not – be used. Both the BBC and IBA have from time to time graded words according to their offensiveness. In a recent ruling 'bollocks' was not approved before nine o'clock but, curiously, 'bugger' and 'piss off' were all right in small doses. 'Shag' was only allowable before nine if it referred to tobacco or the common cormorant. 'Fuck' could not be said at all.

Times change. Some children's dramas – meaningful, socially relevant ones – now sometimes include phrases like 'piss off' and words like 'arsehole', while 'fuck off' is heard on terrestrial television after nine o'clock. Satellite television now shows feature films that have not been expurgated.

The new writer needs a good story and good dialogue – but providing it is justified, the use of gutsy language will not do any harm. A few 'bollocks' will meet with most script editors' approval – it gives them something to champion, and lets them think they are advancing the cause of television drama. And at the end of the day they can always cut them out.

COMMON FAULTS IN DIALOGUE

Unsayable lines

New writers often write dialogue that looks fine on paper, but is actually very difficult to say. Read your lines out loud to see how well they work. Avoid not only tongue twisters like 'the Leith Police dismisseth us', but convoluted lines, repetitive lines, and lines with a great number of very short words: 'I'll just ask if they don't mind us going out to find out what was going on.' (Mind you, if you do write a line as bad as that you might as well give up.)

This is not to say you can't repeat words and phrases:

> DICK: OK, all right, that's it then Sunbeam, you've done it this time, this time you are in real trouble, oh yes you are in *real* trouble...

says our angry policeman moving rapidly across the cell and grabbing his victim by the throat.

Dialogue should be alive, it should sparkle. It has been described as the 'nerve ends of feelings', it is usually based on emotional responses, and if it is well written it gives pace and energy to the script.

Use of dialect

It is risky to get enmeshed in dialect and foreign accents. A play written in dialect is pretty well guaranteed to make a script editor's eyes glaze over. Italians crying 'Mama Mia' and Frenchmen shouting 'Allez mes enfants!' are nearly as off-putting as Yorkshiremen saying 'Ahm gerrin off down't pit but a'l sithi' in't mornin''. Regional clichés ('By gum, it's a bit parky tonight, mother') are also best avoided, and the example of dialogue below not only shows us the awfulness of fake dialect but also demonstrates another fault common in many scripts:

GEORGE: Shall us have our tea now then Martha?

MARTHA: Aye if tha's ready George.

GEORGE: Wilt have an egg wi' bacon for tha's tea Martha?

MARTHA: If that's what tha's havin', George.

GEORGE: Ah thinks ah'll have a sausage, Martha.

MARTHA: You have what tha' bloody well likes, George.

The additional fault is:

Overuse of character names

A common fault is for characters to call each other by name to an extent that is not credible. In real life we rarely need to tag a person's name on to the end of a sentence, and in conversation most people only use a person's name to create intimacy or to emphasise the importance of what they are saying. A woman might say: 'John, that is not true. I swear to you that I was nowhere near Randy Ron's house last night', or a man might say: 'I'm sorry Michele, I really am.'

Pseudo dialect, badly chosen character names (see page 72) and overuse of character names can ruin dialogue that might otherwise be perfectly acceptable. Look at the dialogue between George and Martha if the dialect is taken out, the characters given different names and the passage put in a dramatic framework.

GILLIAN's nerves are at breaking point. Her father-in-law TOM has been staying in the house since the death of her husband PATRICK in an accident three weeks ago. TOM is a widower in his late eighties, bewildered and lost – GILLIAN tries to be kind, but all she wants is to be alone.

GILLIAN sits staring into the empty fireplace. TOM looks at her once or twice.

TOM: Shall we have some tea?

GILLIAN: If you're ready.

She does not move. TOM says nothing for a moment, then tries to speak brightly.

TOM: Will you have some eggs and bacon?

GILLIAN: If that's what you're having.

She still does not look up.

TOM: I think I'll have a sausage.

GILLIAN: Have what you bloody well like!

Silence. Slowly, GILLIAN starts to cry.

SUMMARY

- Every line of dialogue should advance the story, reveal the character of the person speaking, or give us background information. A good line will do all three things.
- Every word you write should be necessary or should be cut.
- Dialogue should sound totally natural unless you are writing in a deliberately stylised manner (not recommended: script editors will simply think that you can't write).
- The more you can make your dialogue fresh, lively and vivid the better.
- Avoid dialect.
- Avoid over-using character names.
- Say lines out loud, or in your head, as you write them.

> Writing film and TV plays – that is writing dramatic dialogue – absolutely demands that the writer should be *alive to the sound of everyday speech.*
>
> (Rodney Bennett, director)

8

Chacterisation

GIVING CHARACTERS DEPTH

A common note of dismissal on rejected scripts is: 'characters two dimensional' or 'cardboard characters'. This means that the characters do not 'come off the page' as rounded, interesting, individual personalities. It is not always easy to give characters depth when everything they do, or say, must somehow advance the story. Here are some hints:

- Avoid stereotypes. For example, do not have retired colonels who cry 'What? What?' in peppery voices and complain about young people today.
- Give even minor characters more than one aspect to their nature. This does not have to be extreme – you do not have to give a vicar a penchant for roulette and girls – but remember that people are made up of a complex mixture of likes, dislikes, strengths, weaknesses and moral views.
- At its simplest, if you have a postman who appears two or three times in your script, and whose only function is to deliver letters critical to your plot, decide: Is he a happy postman? Or a miserable postman? Does he perhaps whistle, and if so, what sort of tune? A whistling postman is a bit of a cliché, but what if he's a dour, miserable-looking postman who always whistles 'The Sun has got his hat on, hip-hip-hip-hurray?' You will, *without a single line of dialogue*, have given your postman an intriguing feature, a personality.
- A cunning if weary old ploy used by professional writers is to give the hero a minor failing (a detective hero who can't resist cream buns) and the villain a minor virtue (a gangster with a secret passion for Gilbert and Sullivan operettas). This technique can give the script the appearance, at least, of depth of characterisation.

- You can sometimes rescue a clichéd character late on in a script by adding unexpected humour and self-awareness. Your peppery colonel mutters 'Dear God, young people today! His wife says, 'Why do you *always* have to say that?' He replies musingly, 'I've no idea. Perhaps because it's expected of me', and his wife stares at him in amazement. This technique gives you the advantage of the stereotype (viewers know exactly where they are) with the added virtue of dramatic revelation as a new side to the colonel's character is revealed.

DEVELOPING CHARACTERS

The development of character is an important part of any drama – indeed, most dramas are not about action but about reaction, not about car chases and murder but about the effect such events have on the attitudes of the people who survive them.

The important thing is to build the different facets of a person's personality into a coherent whole. The actor studying the part will be looking for a **through line** of character development (see page 63). If the character in question is mild and sensible at the beginning of the play, but ends up smashing the furniture and butchering the cat, then the actor will:

- want to know why his character has changed
- want to understand the thought processes that have led to the change
- look for the key line, possibly by another character ('People forget George's unpredictable temper, but it's always there, it's not gone away') that will help to understand why he has turned into a cat-murdering fiend
- go back to the beginning – and create a performance from the start which allows the character later to reveal hidden emotional depths.

Actors become frustrated when they find in one scene that they are good-natured, and in another scene that they are not – but cannot find any explanation in the script.

ILL-TREATING CHARACTERS

Writers can do terrible things to their characters. They create creatures that live and breathe – and then destroy them, carelessly or ruthlessly, to maintain their plot, or to save a scene that is looking sticky, or because they can't think what to do next and making a character do something highly peculiar will cause a temporary sensation.

There are two forms of character sacrifice to beware of:

- sacrificing character for plot
- sacrificing character for sensation.

Sacrificing your characters for plot

The most common fault is to make formerly intelligent characters behave stupidly for no reason (see the idiot plot, page 43), or to make characters behave out of character because the plot demands it.

Perhaps your story is that of a 16-year-old girl who is pregnant and who is frightened to tell anyone. You want us to see her attempting to confide in a succession of people, including her mother.

ELVA: The thing is Mum –

MUM: Just look at your father! I don't know what he thinks he's doing!

ELVA: I'm in trouble... real trouble –

MUM: Out there in this wind without his pullover on!

ELVA: I've got to tell you – I'll go mad if I don't tell somebody.

MUM: Just go and give him a shout, Elva – I know I like fresh brussels sprouts but if he gets one of his colds we'll hear about it for weeks.

Mum here is presumably stone deaf and stupid – all very well, but elsewhere in the play we may have found her to be a perfectly normal, reasonably intelligent person. The writer *needs* Elva to fail to communicate so that she can be rejected by the world (and so that the play will run for a full 50 minutes), so in this particular scene Mum's character as a sane human being is sacrificed to make the plot work. A similar occurrence is likely to happen in the doctor's surgery:

ELVA: (Whispers) I'm sorry I've no appointment –

RECEPTIONIST: Twenty past three Wednesday with Dr McClaren.

ELVA: I was hoping this afternoon –

RECEPTIONIST: Sorry, Wednesday's the earliest I can manage. (Phone. She lifts it.) Excuse me. Medical Centre, can I help you?

ELVA turns and goes. The RECEPTIONIST reaches for her appointments book. As ELVA goes out in the dark rainy afternoon we hear:

RECEPTIONIST: (OOV into phone) Can you manage 3.20 on Wednesday with Dr McClaren?

All very well if the intention is to portray the receptionist as unsympathetic – but a problem if we have previously found her to be perceptive and warm hearted with a natural affinity for the young.

Sacrificing your character for sensation

Sacrificing a character on the altar of sensation is a major crime, most commonly done in soap operas. Perhaps a happily married woman suddenly goes berserk and starts having an affair with a character she has previously shown no interest in whatsoever. To understand why, we need to go back to a storyline meeting three months previously.

Producer, editors, storyliners and writers are fretting over what to do with Alice, who has not had a decent story for ages. This is a major crisis – not because the actress concerned is complaining night and day (nobody cares about that) but because she has been guaranteed 20 episodes (or at least payment for 20 episodes) and so far she has only been in three. The storyline meeting must find her a story! In the end somebody says: 'We've no story for George, either. Why don't they have an affair.' Everybody of sense at the meeting says it's impossible, Alice is 48 and president of the Mothers' Union, George is a 21-year-old rock singer. It simply would never happen! But the producer is a desperate woman (it's five minutes to opening time) so she says: 'Anything can happen in life, we mustn't be hidebound.' Alice has her pointless affair and her character is irrevocably altered.

It is easy to get a temporary sensation by making somebody behave oddly, but it does not work unless what happens genuinely springs from within the personality of the character concerned.

THE THOUGHT PROCESS

> A drama ought to bring out character as a photographer's chemicals bring out the forms latent on the negative.
>
> (William Archer)

The film *Three Into One Won't Go* opens with a middle-aged man driving his car. He comes across a very attractive girl thumbing a lift. He stops, some distance beyond her, opens the car door, and waits for her to come and jump in. When he looks back she is standing, hand on hip, waiting for him to back up to her. Unsmiling, he backs the car, and she gets in.

Not a word of dialogue has been spoken, but already we know of his middle-aged sexual frustration, and of her self-assurance and knowledge of the power she has over men of a certain age.

You cannot write for a character unless you know that character and understand what they are thinking at all times. When a character says something you always need to know why, because when an actor plays the part he must have a reason for what he is saying and doing. If you do not supply one, then the actor will have to find his own.

This sounds obvious – of course a writer knows what a character is thinking – but it is far from uncommon for a frustrated and simmering actor to corner a helpless writer after a read-through and say: 'I just cannot understand why I say this line on page 19: "Higgs deserves promotion if anybody does", when on page 5 I nodded in agreement when Jones said that Higgs was a brain-dead idle prat. Am I telling a complete lie? I mean, I can, of course, if that's what you intend.'

'Yes, that's it,' says the desperate writer, his mouth full of chicken vol-au-vent, but the actor continues remorselessly: 'But of course it totally affects the way I say the line, and if I'm lying why do I tell Sarah on page 24 that Higgs is the best thing that ever happened to the school?'

CHARACTER NAMES

When did you ever find a wicked Mary?
(BBC drama script editor)

A respected series writer had one failing. She could never think up a name for the new characters she had to introduce. She would ponder for hours, but her characters always ended up being called Robinson – usually Jim Robinson or Bill Robinson. A special effort might yield Robertson, and one day she even managed a Roberts. It was always left to the script editor to think up something different.

Names are strangely important – particularly Christian names. Given that in real life our personalities and names are connected in a totally arbitrary fashion, one ought to be able to produce six names for six characters and then shuffle them in a bag. But it does not work like that. See if you agree with the following.

- Hard names go with hard personalities; soft names with good-natured people.
- Working-class characters are called Bert and Maureen, toffs are called Simon and Emma.
- Young working-class characters are called Wayne and Sharon, young toffs are still called Simon and Emma.
- Working classes are surnamed Grice and Leech and Stott, toffs are surnamed Burlington-Smythe and Pomeroy and Beauchamp.

These are the clichés. But in real life, of course, the clichés are often true. You won't find many hereditary peers called Wayne or peeresses called Kylie, and if you shout 'Jeremy' or 'Henrietta' on a Toxteth housing estate you won't hear the patter of many tiny feet.

It is also true that the public has expectations from certain names, and the dramatist can use them as tools of his trade. A psychological study in America revealed that desirable names included Gregory and Craig; unpopular, undesirable names included Elmer, Hubert, Darrell and Horace. In Britain all the above names might be considered unappealing. A British report in the 1980s found that the public regard:

- John as trustworthy
- Robin as young
- Tony as sociable

- Agnes as old
- Ann as non-aggressive
- William as steady.

Names to help portray character

Some of the greatest writers have created names that contain within themselves the essence of the people they describe. David Copperfield's stepfather's sister was Miss Murdstone and the stolid carter was Barkis ('Barkis is willin'').

Imagine the names changed about, with the hero David Barkis, the horrid stepfather's sister Miss Copperfield, and the carter murmuring 'Murdstone is willin''.

The trick is to devise names that sound *appropriate* and at the same time avoid the obvious cliché. Jobbing gardeners should not be called Mr Potts – but neither should they be called Fossington-Fawcett (unless there is a deliberate irony, as when you call a pigman Lavender). Dashing, sexy heroes called Raymond Witson or Terry Stott or Kenneth Swindon are facing an uphill struggle, but so are Rik Steele and Jed Tempest.

Names to add colour

Names can be memorable (Dr Strangelove) or likeable and affectionate (Hawkeye and Trapper). The most important thing is that they should stand out (avoid too many characters called Smith and Brown and Tom and Fred) and should roll off the tongue in a satisfying way (Ena Sharples, Annie Walker).

And some to avoid

Avoid names that are similar – a Johnny and a Ronnie, a Mandy and a Sandy – in the same play.

SUMMARY

- Characters must have more than one characteristic.

- Avoid stereotypes.

- Do not force characters to behave stupidly in order to make a creaking plot work.

- Do not allow characters to behave out of character without reason or explanation.

- Remember that everything a character says or does reveals an aspect of their personality.
- Avoid cliché names.

> Every single character, even a bastard like Goldberg in *The Birthday Party*, I care for.
>
> (Harold Pinter)

9

Situation Comedy

Situation comedies – sitcoms – are commonly thought to be the hardest scripts of all to write. The problem – as one ITV Head of Comedy put it – is that whilst you can generally get some kind of broad agreement about the merits of a straight drama script, it is virtually impossible to find agreement over what is or is not funny.

The chemistry of the production is also vital and unpredictable. Sometimes scripts and actors seem brilliant, but the result, after rehearsal and recording, is dull, plodding and deadly. On the other hand a script thought desperately weak might suddenly take off when the cast and director get to work on it.

It's a difficult area of writing, but the rewards are high if you can get it right. In this chapter we look at:

- the different types of comedy
- stories in sitcom
- characters in sitcom
- structure in sitcoms
- to joke or not to joke?
- budgets
- hints for the new sitcom writer
- hit comedies.

THE DIFFERENT TYPES OF COMEDY

The most common reason for scripts being rejected – apart from them being simply not funny on any level – is that they mix different styles, and thus fail at all of them. As a new writer, you need to be very clear from the beginning about the type of comedy you are writing.

Suspended disbelief

In sitcoms like *Blackadder* or *'Allo 'Allo* we happily suspend our disbelief. In other words we don't mind characters doing bizarre, illogical things or reacting to events in a way that would be unbelievable in rational human beings. When Baldrick spends a fortune on a turnip we don't say: 'This is ridiculous, no turnip could cost that much, and if it did surely Mr Blackadder would at least look surprised...' If we do say this sort of thing we are clearly humourless and our spouse will divorce us, and our pets will all seek new homes.

Comedies that incorporate the absurd are the most difficult to get right. All comedy involves a deviation from the norm, and if there are no rules of normal behaviour it is hard to get a laugh out of people deviating from them.

Comedy of wit and logic

In a programme like *Yes, Prime Minister* we are presented with a basically unbelievable situation: a not-very-bright prime minister willing to devote hours each day to being outwitted by one obviously manipulative civil servant. But once the unreality of the premise is accepted, the scripts are totally logical and the two characters completely rational and believable. Similarly in *The Brittas Empire* well-drawn characters react with perfect logic as the situations become more and more ludicrous. *Fawlty Towers* is the classic: supreme in that every story depends on the remorseless logic of the bizarre situations created.

Comedy of life

From *The Good Life* to *A Fine Romance* to *Absolutely Fabulous* comedies about believable people doing unusual, interesting or just well-observed things have been hugely successful. These comedies are essentially about the way people live, about ambitions and hopes. We are not required to suspend our disbelief when we watch them – or at least, only a little bit.

Broken comedy

This is sketch-type comedy, examples being *French and Saunders* and *Harry Enfield and Chums*.

STORIES

There is little agreement over appropriate stories between the programme makers. Comedies that open with the reading of a will, or the winning of the lottery, are said to be clichés – but that doesn't mean you won't see both on screen in 12 months time. For post-watershed showing, BBC 1 wants 'sophisticated, distinctive comedy which is adult in ambition and tone' – and gives as an example *Men Behaving Badly*. For pre-watershed showing it wants programmes that have 'inclusiveness and a sense of community'.

Channel 4 is happiest when its comedies have something to say about society hence *The Wilsons* which features single parents and social workers – and with experimental shows that incubate writer-actor talent like *Ali-G* and the all-female *Smack the Pony*.

SETTINGS

Good sitcoms often take a very ordinary setting and then let the characters turn it upside down – suburbia in *One Foot in the Grave*, a seaside hotel in *Fawlty Towers*.

Zany, off-beat situations on the other hand are regarded as notoriously hard to make funny. 'A fish running an Internet café set on the dark side of Mars is not original but desperate,' says the BBC scathingly.

Sitcoms set in the not-too-far-distant past can find favour – the 1970s for *The Grimleys* and the 1960s for *Hippies*.

At the end of the day the setting is not as important as what you, the writer, do with it. 'Flat-sharing' has long been said to be an overworked and clichéd setting – but that didn't stop the BBC 2 hit *Gimme, Gimme, Gimme*.

CHARACTERS

Sitcom characters ought not to be too nice, says the BBC, and by nice they mean bland. Characters in comedy engage our interest because of their flaws not because of their good nature. Captain Mainwaring and Victor Meldrew are likeable, of course, but it is the former's pomposity and the latter's frustration that makes us laugh. Most comedy characters have ordinary characteristics that are heightened. Stupid characters are extra stupid, snobby people are extra snobby. The golden rule is that *characters must be consistent*. In *Blackadder* Baldrick always has a cunning plan, Blackadder is always cynical, and the deeply, if engagingly, stupid character is always deeply and engagingly stupid.

Sitcom is also very much about the **conflict** of characters within the situation you have set up. Conflict situations can include the following.

- **Opposites** – *Friends* gets much of its background comedy from an untidy person sharing a flat with an obsessionally tidy person; and a bloke confident with the opposite sex sharing a flat with a bloke who is insecure with the opposite sex.

- **Role reversal** – in *Absolutely Fabulous* Edina Monsoon is wild and irresponsible, while daughter Saffy is sensible and grown-up. In *The Peter Principle* the middle-aged bank manager is incompetent and loopy, his young female assistant is competent and in control.

STRUCTURE

The structure of a sitcom is the same as that for any other kind of drama. (Crisis. Confusion. Resolution.) Typically in a sitcom, however, there will be a final twist to the end.

1. You set up a crisis.
2. The crisis deepens as your principal characters try – hilariously if possible – to resolve it.
3. They believe they have finally succeeded.
4. They suddenly find that they haven't.

The final stage might only last for four seconds – time for the ceiling to collapse, the studio audience to roar, and the signature tune to play loudly as we go chortling into the credits.

TO JOKE OR NOT TO JOKE?

The BBC in particular has an aversion to jokes and 'one-line gags'. You should not try to make every line a laugh, they say, severely, but should create humour out of characters reacting to comic situations with actions and dialogue. In other words, the rules of straight drama also apply to comedy. This does not mean you must avoid comic lines like Hancock's 'A pint? Ave you gone mad? That's very nearly an armful!' in *The Blood Donor*.

At the end of the day all you can do is write what you yourself believe to be funny. 'Do not simply try to match some mediocre show you saw on TV last night', the BBC warns, probably fearing a thousand proposals based on *My Hero*.

> What we are about primarily is the incubation of new talent…Our audience is not interested in those slightly old-fashioned sitcoms like the BBC's *Beast*, which, though very funny, could have been made in 1978….we're looking for comedy that feels different.
>
> (Kevin Lygo, Head of Comedy, Channel 4)

BUDGETS

The BBC warns independent producers that high-cost shows – for which there are always many, many proposals – must be 'balanced by some series at the lower end of the range'. The opportunity for the new writer, therefore, is to present the independent company with something that is beautifully-written, hilariously funny, and cheap. A high-cost sitcom on BBC 1 has a budget of around £230,000 but a show with fewer sets (and thus a smaller studio requirement) little or no recording on location, and no starry actors, would have a budget of around £175,000. This is the slot to aim for.

HINTS FOR THE NEW SITCOM WRITER

- Most successful sitcoms have only three or four central characters.
- Those with a large cast work best when there is a place where the characters can meet and interact without the need to explain what they are doing there. In *Dad's Army* and *The Vicar of Dibley* the characters meet naturally in the church hall; in *Drop the Dead Donkey* they meet in the newsroom.
- A high proportion of sitcoms explore aspects of the British character and the British way of life.
- Most sitcoms are recorded before a live audience, and therefore have only three or four sets.
- Give yourself a theme – i.e. the recurrent theme of *Friends* is the nature of friendship; the theme of *Last of the Summer Wine* is that you don't have to be young to be foolish; the theme of *Men Behaving Badly* is men behaving badly.

- Make sure that your theme – the premise of your situation – has ongoing comic possibilities.
- Few comic ideas can sustain half an hour. Consider having two or three stories running at once – they don't necessarily have to interweave, though it is regarded as neat if the outcome of one story alters or shapes the outcome of another.
- Surprise and outwit your audience. The classic example provided by Charlie Chaplin was: A man walks along a street. The camera cuts to a banana skin on the pavement. The audience expect the man to slip on it – but instead he carefully steps over it, looks back at it with a smile, and promptly falls down a manhole.
- Avoid spending the first dozen pages of your script introducing the characters and setting the scene. For some reason this always involves over-acting, feeble jokes, and forced humour. Start your episode with a *strong story* that gives the actors something to act, and makes us want to know what happens next. Even better: describe the set-up, give a synopsis of the first two or three episodes, and then write and submit the episode that follows on.
- Humour has to be sustained. American sitcom producers aim to trigger a laugh every 13 seconds.
- But don't force the humour. It must arise naturally from the situation you have skilfully created (in between your 13-second laughs).
- Sitcom writing often works well as a joint effort – two writers exchanging ideas and rewriting each others' draft scripts.
- Don't write for a specific star actor, even if you have an ideal actor in mind. The production companies want to see how you write original comedy for characters of your own creation.
- Go and watch a sitcom being made. For information on BBC sitcoms phone (020) 8576 1227, look at the website *www.bbc.co.uk/tickets* or write to:

  BBC Audience Services
  Room 301 Design Building
  BBC Television Centre
  London W1R 7RJ

- Take advantage of online comedy workshops. They are run from time to time by the BBC, Channel 4, Carlton, and independent companies (see Chapter 18).

HIT COMEDIES

For what it's worth, and to show what comedy afficionados want – which is not necessarily the same as what programme makers want – one 2000 Internet poll to find the most popular British sitcoms came up with a top ten of:

Only Fools and Horses
Dad's Army
As Time Goes By
Keeping Up Appearances
'Allo 'Allo
Absolutely Fabulous
Blackadder
One Foot in the Grave
The Vicar of Dibley
Jeeves and Wooster

> Someone who's never done anything before isn't going to be handed a huge commission. But if writers or performers are inexperienced, the department can find people to work with them. There is money to develop pilots and the Comedy Lab can get talent on air for quite small budgets.
>
> (Channel 4)
>
> If you can't come up with an idea just stick some kids in it, it never fails. 'My Son the Boss' – you work in a crazy company where your son is the boss, it's insane. 'Castaway Kids' – where you adopt some kids who were left on your doorstep. 'Kids in Space' – where you adopt some kids who were left on your doorstep by aliens.
>
> (American writer Andy Kindler)

10

Presentation

HOW TO MAKE THE RIGHT IMPRESSION

The all-important moment will come when a script editor or professional reader opens your script at the first page – and instantly forms a judgement. This judgement will be based on the style and presentation of your work. It will be a superficial judgement and a work of quality will shine through the poorest layout. But it makes sense to give a good impression: the impression of a serious writer confident about his work.

PRESENTATION THAT LETS YOU DOWN

Avoid at all costs sending in scripts that are:

- written carelessly
- poorly laid out on the page
- lazily presented
- tired and travel-stained
- written for another medium (e.g. radio)
- professionally 'packaged'.

Careless scripts

Script editors are not impressed by scripts that are carelessly typed with obvious mistakes and characters muddled up:

JOHN
I love you now and I have always loved you.

SALLY
Conviction, John, conviction is what I want to hear.

SALLY
I love you and I have alwoys loved you, dammit!

SALLY
Somehow it still doesn't sund right.

As Sally cannot have three speeches one after another, it is, of course, easy to work out that the middle speech belongs to John. Typing errors are easily explained. But working this out slows up the reading of the script, interrupts the flow of the narrative, and reveals that the writer has not bothered to read his work through before posting it.

'I always write fast – once the idea comes to me I just have to get it down on paper, and once I've written it, that's it, I just can't look at it again.' So says the hopeful writer, presumably believing that the script editor will be impressed or at the very least indulgent.

The script editor will not be impressed or indulgent. The script editor will think: 'This is an amateur wasting my time.'

Poor layout on the page

Avoid layout that is confusing or unfamiliar, or makes it hard to separate dialogue from studio directions. Do not write:

John 'Good Morning'
Jane 'Good morning, darling. What do you want for breakfast'
John 'Egg and bacon please.' John pauses then says 'On second thoughts I'll just have coffee.'
Jane shakes her head. Jane 'You and your silly diet'
John sits down and hides behind his copy of the paper. He is annoyed by Jane mentioning his weight again. I see the West Indies are all out for ninety five.
Jane 'You know I never read cricket.'

Scripts do arrive written like this, and the prejudice against them is considerable. The script editor assumes, reasonably, that if the writer cannot be bothered to consider the basic principles of script layout – or even to be consistent in the style he has chosen – then he has little chance of ever succeeding in the demanding, professional world of television.

Lazy presentation

A surprisingly large number of new writers use initials for the names of characters rather than spelling them out each time the character speaks. The writer tells us on the first page that his characters are called Henry and June and have two children called Kylie and Tom. In the script itself he writes:

H: I want everybody in the car in five minutes.
K: I can't find my cosie! Where's my cosie!
J: I haven't the foggiest idea, but I do know I told you to start looking for it three hours ago.
T: I've got mine. I always know where mine is.

Script editors hate this. They keep having to refer back to the front page to remind themselves who T is and who K is. This makes it hard for them to become absorbed in your work.

Tired and travel-stained script

Do not submit scripts that are:

- world-weary, crumpled and yellowing with age
- have comments on them from a previous submission.

Do not expect wonderful results from scripts that are creased and curly at the corners, decorated with ancient coffee stains, festooned with little messages like 'Ack 27/3/94' and with comments in the margins: 'Does not follow', 'Who is this character?', 'Weak dialogue' or even, showing the ultimate boredom, some previous script reader's shopping list. These are the signs of a well-travelled script that has seen the world and knows what it is to be rejected. It is a script that expects, even as the editor lifts it gingerly from her 'unsolicited' tray, to be rejected again. And it is.

> A script must read clearly and easily as a piece of narrative; it must show its quality not only as a piece of writing, but as a piece of television writing.
>
> (Arthur Swinson)

Scripts written for another medium

If you have had no luck with a radio play and decide to try it on television – fine. But make sure you adapt it first. There is no point in sending a radio play to a television company with the hopeful plea: 'Although this is written for radio, I now think it would be very good on television.' Few editors will bother to read it. You might just as well make a chair and try to sell it to somebody who wants a table.

If you do adapt a radio play, check it carefully before you send it off. All too often, around page six or seven, can be found the tell-tale sound direction: 'Fade up grams FX of storm at sea'.

It is also common for writers to adapt a play from television to radio, and still to leave in directions for cameras to pan, or cut, or zoom. Radio producers loath this. They feel inferior enough already, without people conning them into buying television drama's rejects.

Overkill presentation

Some writers go to endless trouble getting their script typed by a professional agency, often with the title printed via the magic of desktop publishing, and the result bound lavishly like a Hollywood studio script.

It seems heartless to say to a writer so obviously making an effort 'Don't bother' – but it is a mistake to spend too much time concentrating on presentation. Nobody is going to buy a script because it comes in a lavish presentation package. Many script editors will be actively put off.

There is a feeling that the script has already been 'processed' in some way, or that it is being dressed up smart to cover its inadequacies. The script editor, remember, is sustained by the hope that the next unsolicited script she reaches for will be a work of genius – a first offering by the Dennis Potter or Simon Gray of the future.

Somehow nobody expects genius to come in a glitzy, professional presentation.

> There is a perverse rule of thumb amongst editors and producers in British television that the more impeccably the script is presented, the duller the contents.
>
> (Eric Paice, writer)

PRESENTATION THAT HELPS YOU

Things to think about here are:

- page layout
- writing for the camera
- writing for the actor.

Page layout

Some new writers worry endlessly about layout. They know that television scripts wastefully use only half of the page, and that there is a mysterious professional code governing the use of CAPITAL letters for characters' names, and that colons and underlinings feature strangely, and that professional scripts are dotted with terse instructions demanding an MCU or a 2-SHOT or a PAN LEFT. (See Chapter 17, TV Talk.)

In fact, there is no fixed layout even among production scripts, which vary between the BBC and ITV companies and in small details often follow the personal whim of the production secretary. Certainly at the first stage of writing there are no vital formulae, and as you are not typing a studio script it is pointless to imitate one.

That said, it is common sense to conform to a layout that will be familiar to the script editor, and will be easy to read and to understand. Two of the basic rules are:

- always make a clear distinction between dialogue and description
- always leave a wide margin on the left-hand side of the page.

What you are trying to achieve is a simple, straightforward layout that will allow the reader or script editor to read your play effortlessly, gripped by your story, intrigued by your characters and savouring your excellent dialogue.

There are two basic layouts. They have one thing in common: they are easy to read, and they are familiar to script editors, readers and directors alike. (See Figures 1 and 2.)

Writing for the camera

Should you indicate when you want a medium close up (called an MCU)? Or a two-shot? Or when you think the use of a crane shot or dolphin arm might be of artistic use? The answer is no, don't do any of these things unless they are vital to the telling of your story. Script editors find they get in the way, writers get bogged down in technicalities and end up thinking they have written a professional script just because it *looks* like a professional script.

It is not your job to write a camera script, it is your job to write a play.

At the same time you need to write with the camera in mind, and it is quite legitimate for you to indicate a camera move *if it is important to the telling of your story.*

Suppose you are writing a play about a doctor investigating the effect of a sinister new drug on blood cell structure. You want to open a scene with the screen filled with pictures of the drug molecules killing helpless blood cells, while a character tells excitedly of the discovery she has made.

1. EXT. FRONT GARDEN OF CROSSLEY HOUSE. EARLY MORNING

The front door opens and the family Rottweiler CONAN is let out into the garden.

BOBBY (OOV)
Go on, get out!

The front door closes. CONAN trots to the front gate and looks out. A dirty and rather old Ford escort is parked on the other side of the road.

2. INT. UNMARKED POLICE CAR. EARLY MORNING

DC ROBERTS, the passenger, stares across the road at CONAN.

ROBERTS
That's the best looking member of the family I've seen so far.

DC LAWLESS, the driver, peeps from behind his Sun.

ROBERTS
It looks almost intelligent, comparatively.

LAWLESS folds his paper and starts the car.

LAWLESS
Time for breakfast.

ROBERTS
It's the eyes, there's something behind them, that's what makes the difference.

3. INT. BOBBY CROSSLEY'S BEDROOM. EARLY MORNING

BOBBY is watching the car drive down the road.

BOBBY
Bastards.

Fig. 1. Script layout: style one.

47. EXT. CROSSLEYS FRONT GARDEN. NIGHT

TWO POLICE OFFICERS WEARING BLACK WITH BLACK NYLON BALACLAVAS MOVE TOWARDS THE MOTORBIKE. THE SECOND KEEPS WATCH AS THE FIRST STARTS TO FIX A BLACK BOX TO THE UNDERSIDE OF THE BIKE.

48. EXT. CROSSLEYS BACK YARD. NIGHT

CONAN GETS UP AND LISTENS.

49. EXT. CROSSLEYS FRONT GARDEN. NIGHT

POLICEMAN ONE IS FIDDLING WITH THE BOX.

50. EXT. CROSSLEYS BACK YARD. NIGHT

CONAN MOVES TOWARDS THE FRONT OF THE HOUSE

51. EXT. CROSSLEYS FRONT GARDEN. NIGHT

CONAN APPEARS FROM THE BACK YARD. HE GROWLS

POLICEMAN TWO: (Whisper) Dog!

POLICEMAN ONE: Sodding hell, I thought you said it was inside for the night.

CONAN GETS CLOSER AND MORE ANNOYED LOOKING. POLICEMAN TWO GETS A LUMP OF PIPING FROM INSIDE HIS LEATHER JACKET. CONAN LOOKS AT HIM.

POLICEMAN ONE: Do something about it.

POLICEMAN TWO CLUMPS CONAN OVER THE HEAD WITH THE PIPING. CONAN WHIMPERS AND DROPS. POLICEMAN ONE STARES DOWN.

POLICEMAN TWO: Get on with it, they'll kill us now if they find us.

POLICEMAN ONE CONTINUES WITH HIS TASK. CONAN IS BREATHING LIKE A DOG WITH A PROBLEM.

Fig. 2. Script layout: style two.

INT. LABORATORY. DAY
The screen is filled with a computer simulation of ZYX cells attacking ABC cells. We hear DR WARD:

WARD (OOV)
They multiply at bloodheat, and within 2.4 seconds they begin to attack. They are deadly and they are irresistible. Your placebo, Professor Smith, is a killer.

CUT TO: WARD and SMITH staring down at the screen. SMITH's face is expressionless.

WARD
You understand why I wanted you to come straight away. I'm sorry.

CUT TO: CU of SMITH staring down. From his POV we move slowly in again on the screen. Eerie theme music plays as we go closer and closer.

WARD (OOV)
Professor Smith? Are you all right?

In this illustration (OOV) indicates that Ward is speaking 'Out of Vision' and CUT TO indicates, as you would expect, that the camera cuts directly to WARD and SMITH. (We could have written PULL BACK instead of CUT TO, and this would have meant that the camera would slowly pull back from the screen to reveal the two characters staring down.) We then go to a CLOSE UP of SMITH before looking at the screen again from SMITH's POV ('Point of View') before the camera zooms slowly down again to a CLOSE UP of the battling blood cells.

These camera directions are quite acceptable as a way of telling your story. The director is unlikely to follow them when the programme is made – he will regard it as a point of honour to shoot the scene differently – but at least you will have shown your artistic intention.

Camera directions commonly used by writers are as follows:

- POV – meaning we see something from a particular character's point of view.

- CLOSE UP (CU) – meaning the camera is close to something, generally somebody's face unless you indicate otherwise.

- PULL BACK – the camera is in close up and you want to pull back to show more.

- ZOOM IN – generally meaning that the camera moves quickly in on an object or person, although you can ask for a SLOW ZOOM.

- CUT TO – the camera cuts from one scene to another, or from one object to another. You can indicate that you want to cut from one person's face to another to show their reactions, but you are getting dangerously into the director's domain.

- OOV – the camera is showing something but we hear the voice of an actor who is speaking at the *same time* in the same scene.

- VO – the camera is showing a scene but we hear the 'Voice Over' of an actor who is not in the scene but might be narrating a story or recalling something in retrospect.

There are more television terms in Chapter 17, but generally speaking experienced writers leave pointing the camera to the person who's paid to point it – the director.

Writing for the actor

Actors have two major hates: not having a through line of thought (much more about this in Chapter 7), and being told how they should feel at any particular moment.

GEORGE
(Playfully)
I thought you said you hadn't bought a new dress.

JOANNA
(Angrily)
I haven't bought a new dress, I've had this for ages.

GEORGE
(Tongue in cheek)

That's impossible, it's the very latest fashion (cunningly devious) or perhaps my love, you would make any dress seem to be the latest fashion.

JOANNA
(Fondly)
Oh George, oh do you really think so?

Some actors will tell you that 'mood directions' kill any chance they might have of building a scene during rehearsals, of developing moods themselves and finding their own moments of dramatic tension. They will tell you that if a script *needs* constant pointers as to mood then there is something wrong with it. They will say there is nothing worse than working on lines, creating a scene with a fellow actor, discovering from the text the thoughts and intentions of the character they are playing and then suddenly finding that – for no reason they can fathom – they are supposed to say a line 'Whimsically' or 'Laughingly'.

The trouble is that not all actors are intelligent. There is a world of difference between:

JULIAN
(Acidly)
Well done. What a genius you are my dear.

and

JULIAN
(Warmly)
Well done. What a genius you are my dear.

And not every actor can be relied upon to know how you, the writer, intended it to be spoken. See how the above scene reads quite differently if we change the mood indicators.

GEORGE
(Sharply)
I thought you said you hadn't bought a new dress.

JOANNA
(Wearily)
I haven't bought a new dress, I've had this for ages.

GEORGE (Coldly) That's impossible, it's the very latest fashion (cutting) or perhaps, my love, you would make any dress seem to be the latest fashion.

JOANNA (Sarcastic) Oh George, oh do you really think so.

Writers cannot afford to trust actors entirely. Certainly not in soap operas and series where lines are being learned and performed very quickly. Many actors would not spot that a line was meant to be ironic if you hit them over the head with it, and no writer in his right mind trusts a television director to understand his script.

If you feel you need to indicate a mood at a given time, do so. If the script editor disagrees when she reads the script she will cross it out. Otherwise it will go through and, with luck, the actor will do what you want him to do.

11

From Script to Screen

TURNING A SCRIPT INTO A PROGRAMME

Here we look at how a long-running serial drama is made – from the initial idea, through the storyline stage, and through the different script stages and into production.

Jupiter Moon was a co-production made in 1990/1991 by an independent production company, Primetime Andromeda, for British Satellite Broadcasting and Axel Springer of Germany. One hundred and fifty episodes were recorded and are still being shown in over 30 countries worldwide, from Canada and Greece to Syria and Zimbabwe.

How writers are contacted for serial dramas

Jupiter Moon used several new writers. The script department worked to the following system which is common to most long-running serial dramas.

1. Script editors contact writers they have worked with in the past, and suggest that they read the programme's Guide for Writers and send in a trial script sample. Writers with a track record are paid to write a sample script, writers from another medium (i.e. novels, radio) are sometimes expected to write a half-episode without a fee.

2. Agents (see page 150) are approached and told that the programme is looking for writers who can:

   - write a strong narrative with good pacy dialogue
   - write humour – not sitcom humour but the humour of human relationships
   - have an interest in the particular programme's background, i.e. science fiction for *Jupiter Moon*.

3. New writers who telephone or write are usually asked to send in

an example of their previous work. If this is interesting they will be asked to submit story ideas and/or write half a trial script (without fee). If this is greeted with enthusiasm they will be commissioned to write a single episode, and invited to their first script meeting.

Writers, therefore, come through personal contact, through agents, or by approaching the programme directly. Over the following pages (Figures 3–20) we see what happens next...

SUMMARY

- The writer is commissioned.
- The Guide for Writers describes what the programme is about and includes character breakdowns.
- Writers new to the programme are given guidance notes.
- The Storyline is distributed to writers after the storyline meeting.
- The script comes in from the writer.
- The script is sent to the specialist adviser – who adds his own notes and comments.
- The rehearsal script is typed up and distributed.
- The Props department goes through the script and makes a list of props needed for each scene.
- A requisition is made for food requirements.
- Special effects for the studio are ordered – anything from snow or fireworks to cobwebs and explosions.
- The director orders the graphics he will need.
- The PA breaks down the scenes and makes a brief note of what happens in each scene.

- The actors get their call times for wardrobe and make up.
- A studio script is marked with camera moves.
- The PA notes the running time of each scene – from the first rehearsal through to the Producer's Run, the studio, and the edit.
- After the studio the sound effects are dubbed on to the tape.
- Transmission details are sent to the broadcasting station.

Confidential   Contract Number..003.....

AN AGREEMENT made the sixth day of October 1989 between PRIMETIME ANDROMEDA LIMITED whose registered office is 401, St. Johns Street, London EC1V 4LH (hereinafter referred to as "Primetime Andromeda") of the one part and JULIAN SPILSBURY of Warwickshire hereinafter referred tu as "The Writer") of the other part.

WHEREBY IT IS AGREED as follows:-

Primetime Andromeda hereby commissions The Writer and The Writer accepts the commission to write and deliver the scripts/script (hereinafter referred to as "The Work") detailed in the table below in consideration of the basic fees/fee payable in accordance with the table below and subject to the attached terms and conditions.

DETAILS OF THE SCRIPTS/SCRIPT COMPRISING THE WORK

DESCRIPTION	PROGRAMME TITLE	APPROXIMATE DURATION	BASIC FEE
To write episodes 3, 6, 11, 12, 16, 23, & 24 for the series	"JUPITER MOON"	25 minute slot time	£ 1650.00 x7 £11550.00

DELIVERY DETAILS		TABLE OF PAYMENTS		
SCRIPT	DATE DUE	No.	WHEN DUE	AMOUNT
First and final drafts	between October and 18th December 1989	1	ON INDIVIDUAL COMMISSION	50%
		2.	ON ACCEPTANCE OF EACH SCRIPT	50%

The rewrite of each script must be delivered within SEVEN DAYS of notification to The Writer by the Programme Producer/Script Editor of a requirement for said rewrite

All fees payable to The Writer hereunder shall be payable to Julian Spilsbury whose receipt thereof shall be a complete and valid discharge of Primetime Andromeda's liability

Fig. 3. The writer is commissioned – in this case an experienced writer is commissioned for several episodes.

2

Introduction

JUPITER MOON is a serial drama about life in a space college in the year 2050. Although aimed at a young, intelligent audience it is not designed to be a "cult" space/science programme but to be a programme that will appeal to general viewers.

150 half hour episodes are being made between January 1990 and January 1991. Special effects and OB are being be filmed at Barrandov Studios, Prague, but the bulk of the programme is being recorded at Central Television Facilities, Birmingham.

JUPITER MOON is made by independent production company Primetime-Andromeda and has been shown on the Galaxy channel of British Satellite Broadcasting since March 26th, 1990.

The Idea

Columbus College in 2050AD is part of the University of Space, housed in the spaceship ILEA. It is used by the children of European scientists, administrators, and mining engineers working on the moons of Jupiter; and by undergraduates from Earth, Mars, SpaceStation and Moonstation.

The ILEA floats in permanent orbit over Callisto, the outermost of the Galilean moons. By the ship are the wharves and nuclear tugs of a vast space harbour.

Below, on the satellite itself, is the colony "Space City", with its liquid hydrogen plant, its hostel, spaceport, hospital, cafe/restaurant, nightclub and seedy bar.

JUPITER MOON is about the loves, passions, jealousies and ambitions of young people growing up in an alien but exciting environment.... how they mature as they learn to live with responsibility and cope with emotional relationships...

About the courage, fortitude, and occasional disillusion of men and women who have chosen to make new lives many million miles away from Earth... in particular the men and women working on "Daedalus 10" - a project to build man's first "starship" for a 12 year journey outside the Solar System.

Fig. 4. The **Guide for Writers** describes what the programme is about and includes character breakdowns.

17

IMPORTANT RULES FOR WRITERS

If you can stick to the following it helps us enormously at the production end.

Try not to have more than 29 scenes per episode (excluding special effect modelwork sequences)

Use only 12 characters per episode (if you need 13 talk to a script editor.)

Please use the script layout as per the sample at the end of this guide.

Please list the characters used, at the front of the script.

Each script should have between 44 and 47 full pages - if you like to go to a new page for a new scene make proper allowance for the blank sheets.

DON'T send in a genuine first draft. We need a script that you believe is ready to go into production. It should be properly polished, with tightly written stories, perceptive characterisation, and vivid, lively dialogue.

Please try to balance tense action stories with humorous themes and love/human interest themes.

Fig. 5. Writers new to the programme are also given guidance notes.

VOYAGE OF THE ILEA

STORYLINE 24 (cont)

Episode 149: Part One (Cont)

Sara's Story

It's EVA 1 "space mobility" time for SARA and GABY. SARA has been desperately putting it off. She's happy to do the theory and go in the Zero Chamber - but not outside the ship! REBECCA says: "You've got to do it! What's the point in coming all the way to Jupiter System and never setting foot outside the ship?" Now SARA thinks it will have to be put off again because the Ilea is approaching Jupiter's magnetic field. She is quite cheery. Then DRUMMOND tracks her down. EVA space mobility is on!

GABY chats like an old campagner - she's been out on G33, she's been to Simpson Base! SARA is terrified. So, too, really, is GABY.

The Ship

VICTORIA joins DANIEL on the bridge. Petra announces: "Mercedes Page wishes everyone on the Ilea to know that her Engagement to Professor Charles Bonapart Brelan is cancelled, and invites all her friends to a celebration drink in the Club Galileo at 2100 hrs." DANIEL says: "Is it true about you and Brelan?". VICTORIA says: "Would you be surprised?" DANIEL: "You've always been the serious one." VICTORIA says: "I'm the one who couldn't stand change - I hated my Dad for making me come to Space, but I couldn't not come with him..."

"But you're the one going to Arial 9 - to swim in that ocean perhaps...walk a Mediterranian shore with no people, no pollution.. just sand and sea and sky" - "and little green men!"

A small surge in magnetic force. "Oi oi, better get them in." "Funny the forward opic sensors didn't react."

DRUMMOND in. Computer re-routing. The ship now entering the magnetopshere.... flashing lights.

The dead sentinels spring to life... not flashing amber but red. PETRA issues warning: Red Alert, Red Alert, override, override... and the ship heels as it goes to emergency burn. (Commercial Break)

Fig. 6. The **Storyline** is distributed to writers after the storyline meeting.

4

JIM reaches for his autosec. ANNA grabs her dressing gown and staggers to the shower.

JIM
Petra, Red Spot Radio.

Music blares.

2. COMCEN

DRUMMOND just sitting down. On screen radar sweep with ALL SYSTEMS ON AUTOMATIC over it in green.

DRUMMOND
Petra Systems and Met summary.

PETRA
Good Morning, Commander.

DRUMMOND
Good morning Petra.

PETRA
All shipboard systems nominal. We are on course to intercept with Hymalia in 17 hours 50. Metsat Ayola 9 reports ionised hydrogen and sulphur plumes (Doug help!!!)

REBECCA IN

REBECCA
Why does my heart sink when metsats go on about sulphur plumes.

DRUMMOND
Scale four. We won't even notice. What are you doing up?

REBECCA
Petra what woke me up at 0500 hours?

Fig. 7. The script comes in from the writer – this is the generally accepted layout.

JUPITER MOON — EPISODE 149

6th January 1991

Scene 5 page 12

SARA The Jovian Magnetosphere is the largest in the Solar System...

OK. But for absolute accuracy, add the word 'planetary'

SARA The Jovian planetary Magnetosphere is the largest in the Solar System...

— thus implicitly eliminating the Sun from the comparison

Scene 9 page 22

re: Bow shock and magnetosheath. Someone has been reading up! Congrats to Rowena Rumble I presume

---

Scene 9 page 23

DRUMMOND We didn't pass through Io's flux tube at the same time. 4 million amps, a potential difference of 350,000 volts...

The current is way too high and the voltage would be expressed as a potential difference gradient. But we want high values for what is going to happen in Episode 150. We don't want to use too technical stuff like 'and grad V (∇V) is ...', cos the punters have got to grasp all this. So how about the following?

DRUMMOND We didn't pass through Io's flux tube at the same time. With the plasma eddies you can get effective local currents of 4 million amps, and potential difference gradients of 350,000 volts per centimetre...

Scene 12 page 30

JIM (SHARP) six hundred and eighty six days, Anna. ...

It is actually 686.98 so it's alot closer to 687 as a whole number. Change to 687 if you want to.

Scene 13 page 31

with regards to the pre-breathing. The figure mentioned is 4 litre. That is nowhere

Fig. 8. The script is sent to the scientific adviser – who adds his own notes and comments.

JUPITER MOON

EPISODE ONE HUNDRED & FORTY NINE

WEEK 5	DIRECTOR: David Dunn
EPISODE 149	PA: Fiona Napier
	PRODUCER: William Smethurst
STUDIO	ASSOCIATE PRODUCER: Jane Fallon
29TH, 30TH, 31ST JANUARY	WRITER: Rowena Rumble
	POST PRODUCTION EDITOR: Diane Culverhouse
	SCRIPT EDITOR: Jane Fallon

CAST [in order of appearance]

* PROFESSOR BRELAN	RICHARD DERRINGTON
MERCEDES PAGE	ANNA CHANCELLOR
PETRA (VO)	CHARLOTTE MARTIN
PAUL FITZROY DRUMMOND	RICHARD HAINSWORTH
REBECCA HARVEY	ALISON DOWLING
ANNA BEGANI	ANNA PERNICCI
DANIEL WETHERBY	DANIEL BEALES
VICTORIA FROBISHER	NICOLA WRIGHT
FIONA McBRIDE	LUCY BENJAMIN
SARA ROBBINS	KAREN MURDEN
GABRIELLA TANZI	FAY MASTERSON
JIM HAWKINS	JIM SHEPLEY

PROPERTY OF PRIMETIME ANDROMEDA LIMITED,
CENTRAL TELEVISION STUDIOS,
BROAD STREET,
BIRMINGHAM,
B1 2JP

Fig. 9. The rehearsal script is typed up and distributed.

WEEK 5 EPISODE 149 SCENE 2

SCENE 149.2 INT DAY 2 0730
SET COMCEN

DRUMMOND:	Richard H
PETRA (VO):	Charlotte
REBECCA:	Alison
ANNA (ON SCREEN):	Anna P
MERCEDES (ON SCREEN):	Anna C

DRUMMOND JUST SITTING DOWN. ON SCREEN RADAR SWEEP WITH **'ALL SYSTEMS ON AUTOMATIC'** OVER IT IN GREEN.

DRUMMOND: Petra, Systems and Met summary.

PETRA (VO): Good morning, Commander.

DRUMMOND: (WEARY TOLERANCE) Good morning Petra.

PETRA (VO): All shipboard systems nominal. We are on course to intercept Hymalia in 17 hours 50. Metsat Ayola 9 reports ionised hydrogen and sulphur plumes scale 4 zero zero in Io flux tube, intercept T minus 8 hours forty.

REBECCA IN.

REBECCA: Why does my heart sink when metsats go on about sulphur plumes.

DRUMMOND: Scale four. We won't even notice. What are you doing up?

4

Fig. 10. Layout of the rehearsal script.

M E M O R A N D U M

TO: ALAN BARRETT

FROM: PETER COTTON

DATE: 7th December 1990

cc: Setting Office x 2
Design x 2
FM & AFM's
Props Stores
PA
Director

JUPITER MOON: PROPS REQUIREMENTS: EPISODES 136/137/138

EPISODE 136 (Studio Date): 18th December 1990

SC	SET	PROPS
1	STORAGE ROOM	N/P
2	EXT ILEA	N/P
3	COMCEN	Breakfast ?
4	LONG CORRIDOR	Tim's jacket with food in pockets
5	STORAGE ROOM	Mushroom Quiche ?
6	GANTRY 2 LOBBY	Coffee, Finbow's glasses
7	COMCEN	Finbow's glasses
8	LAB 5	Files, papers etc
9	COMMON ROOM	Breakfast, autosec - Jim
10	LIFT	N/P
11	LECTURE THEATRE	Files, papers etc
12	EXT ILEA	N/P

Fig. 11. The Props department goes through the script and makes a list of props needed for each scene.

M E M O R A N D U M

TO: DAVID WRIGHT - CATERING MANAGER

FROM: PETER COTTON

DATE: 12 DECEMBER 1990

cc: Setting Office x 5
Design x 2
FM + AFM's
PA
Director

JUPITER MOON: PROP FOOD REQUIREMENTS: EPISODES 136/137/138

TUESDAY 18 DECEMBER 1990

3 Doz. Canapes (some to be for a vegetarian)
18 Grilled Mock Halibut Steaks (To look like Salmon)
Tarragon + Cream Sauce (Must be seperate not on fish)
18 Portions of Braised Fennel
18 Portions of Stuffed Aubergines (Vegetarian Stuffing)
48 Profiteroles (Golf Ball Size) (Orange Sauce Seperate- with bits of orange peel in it)
24 Jam Packs
24 Butter Packs

****

WEDNESDAY 19 DECEMBER 1990

Nothing Required

****

THURSDAY 20 DECEMBER 1990

Ass. Salad for 10 people

****

Many thanks

Fig. 12. A requisition is made for food requirements.

Originator

CENTRAL

SPECIAL EFFECTS—
SPECIALITY PROPS REQUIREMENTS

Date Issued 16.12.90 Production a JUPITER MOON Prod No. 8500/137 Date Req. 19.12.90 P.A. SHAN DUCKETT Ext. 4006

RAIN — C.M.	SNOW—Falling —Static — C.M. S.M.	WIND — E.S. L.W.	FOG — C.M. E.S. L.W.	SMOKE — C.M. E.S. L.W. 137.18 - Dome 137.24 - Dome	STEAM — C.M.
COBWEBS — C.M.	B.P.—Still —Moving — C.M. S.M. Proj.	HOUSE APPLIANCES Elec. Prac. — E.S. S.M. L.W.	HOUSE APPLIANCES Gas—prac. — C.M. S.M.	DROP BOXES — C.M.	LAMPS—prac. — S.M. E.S. L.W.
WATER—tanks — S.M. C.M.	WATER—Baths/ Showers — C.M.	WATER—Baths/ Sinks — C.M. Poss.prac hand basin t.b.c 137.1 & 137.3	LAB EFFECTS — C.M.	DRY ICE MACHINE — C.M.	FIRES—Log — C.M.
FIRES—Coal — C.M.	CANDLES—prac. or not — S.M.	EXPLOSIONS — C.M. E.S. L.W.	FLAME EFFECTS — C.M. E.S. L.W.	MACHINE GUN EFFECTS — C.M.	FIREWORKS — C.M. E.S. L.W.
ANIMATED PROPS — C.M.	MAGIC TRICKS/ EFFECTS — C.M. S.M.	FIRE EXTINGUISHERS —prac. — C.M. S.M.	GUNS—practical Non-prac. — C.M. S.M.	BALLOON NETS — C.M.	REVOLVES Turntables — E.S. S.M. L.W.

1. Fill in relevant section giving brief details about effect required.
2. If the effect you require is not specified please use the blank sections.

Fig. 13. Special effects for the studio are ordered – anything from snow or fireworks to cobwebs and explosions.

GRAPHICS SPFX

DIRECTOR HENRY FOSTER

P.A.

EPISODE: 136

EPISODES 136-138

STUDIO 18 - 20 Dec

EDIT 7 - 9 Jan.

SCENE	PAGE	SPFX DESCRIPTION	NEW/ EXISTS	GRAPHICS ACTION REQUIRED	TAPE NO.	TIMECODE
2	8	EXT: SUNRISE OVER GANYMEDE	Exists	no	459	53.50
3	9	COMCEN: General	EXISTS	NO		
7	17	DITTO	"	"		
8	19	LAB 5: DRUMMOND WORKING: Oort cloud?	NEW	YES		
11	26	LECT. THEATRE: Graphics as per page.	NEW	YES		
12	28	EXT: ILEA IN TRANSIT: DAY	EXISTS	NO	757	01.00 - 01.39
13	29	DOME?				
14	32	COMCEN: Scan of ship especially central storage bay hangar. Then hologram of Tim comes up. General scan of ship:	EXISTS?		768	03.25.

Fig. 14. The director orders the graphics he will need.

ENE BREAKDOWN EPISODE 136 jupiter moon 2

SCENE	PAGE	ARTISTES	D/N	OB/ STUDIO	NOTES
136.8	22 to 24	INT LAB 5 REBECCA DRUMMOND MERCEDES	DAY 1 0900	Mercedes decides to invite Drummond & Rebecca to the dinner party	
136.9	25 to 29	INT COMMON ROOM JIM SARA BRELAN MERCEDES	DAY 1 0905	Brelan asks Jim to the prepare the meal for the party but is surprised when Merce tells him it is for 6 people	
136.10	30 to 31	INT LIFT MERCEDES BRELAN	DAY 1 0907	Mercedes asks Brelan if he minds her inviting Drummond & Rebecca to the party	
136.11	32 to 34	INT LECTURE THEATRE JIM DANIEL SARA NS STUDENTS 'MODULE ONE STUDENTS	DAY 1 0930	Daniel is not interested in helping with the party & Jim decides not to move into Cabin 3 with him	
136.12	35 to 35	EXT EXT ILEA	DAY 1 1029	EXT	
136.13	36 to 39	INT DOME JIM SARA ~~AND PLUGS OUT~~	DAY 2 1030	Jim decides what to cook for the d party & Sara decides she will help with the serving	
136.14	40 to 41	INT COMCEN NATASHA PETRA (VO) TIM (HOLO)	DAY 1 1045	Timmy is discovered in the Central Storage bay hangar - Natasha is annoyed	
		End 4 PART			
136.15	42 to 44	INT COMMON ROOM JIM SARA	DAY 1 1930	Jim & Sara start to prepare the meal - Sara is having problem Jim gets annoyed	
136.16	45 to 46	INT BRELAN'S SUITE BRELAN MERCEDES	DAY 1 1944	Brelan gets the drinks ready - Mercedes arrives & Brelan sends her away to get changed	

Fig. 15. The PA breaks down the scenes and makes a brief note of what happens in each scene.

STUDIO CALL TIMES - "JUPITER MOON"

EPISODES 148/149/150

VTR: TUESDAY 29TH JANUARY, 1991

ARTISTE	CHARACTER	WARDROBE	MAKE UP	ON SET
NICOLA WRIGHT	VICTORIA	0800	0830	0900
RICHARD DERRINGTON	BRELAN	0830	0845	0900
JANNA STRIEBECK	TRANQUILITY	0800	0830	0915
ANNA CHANCELLOR	MERCEDES	0800	0830	0930
ALISON DOWLING	REBECCA	0845	0915	1000
CHRISTOPHER SIMON	CHRISTOPHE	0930	0945	1000
FAY MASTERSON	GABRIELLA	0915	0945	1015
JIM SHEPLEY	JIM	0930	0945	1015
LUCY BENJAMIN	FIONA	1000	1030	1100
KAREN MURDEN	SARA	1000	1030	1100
RICHARD HAINSWORTH	DRUMMOND	1045	1100	1115
DANIEL BEALES	DANIEL	1145	1200	1215
ANNA PERNICCI	ANNA	1415	1445	1530

Fig. 16. The actors get their call times for wardrobe and make up.

WEEK 51 EPISODE 136 BLUE SCENE 136.1

TIM: Oh....

TRANQUILITY: I didn't even leave the Transit Lounge, and I didn't give them a chance to get their claws into me/I just slipped off the end of one queue and onto the end of another.

5 4 MCU TIM

TIM: But where are you going to go?/

6 1 MCU TRANQUILITY

TRANQUILITY: Pasiphae, Mars, Earth. Can you hide me somewhere?/

7 4 TIGHT 2 SHOT DEVELOP TO MCU TIM

TIM: But we're going to Ganymede and Hymalia before Pasiphae! We won't get to Pasiphae for weeks.

TRANQUILITY: (PAUSE, THEN) How'd you like to hi-jack a space ship, Timmy?

END OF SCENE

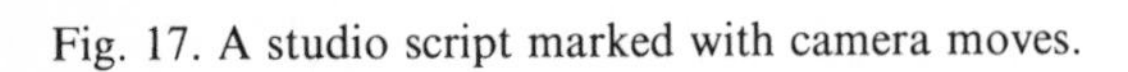

Fig. 17. A studio script marked with camera moves.

JUPITER MOON: EPISODE 137 PN: [illegible]00 VTR: PART ONE

SCENE	READ		FRI		SAT PROD RUN		MON		VTR Edit		EDIT
REPRISE	0025	0025	0025	0025	0025	0025	0025	0025	0058	0058	
OPENING TITLES	0035	0100	0035	0100	0035	0100	0035	0100	0036	0134	
1) CABIN 3	0050	0150	0040	0140	0035	0135	0040	0140	0027	0201	
2) COMCEN	0035	0225	0040	0220	0040	0215	0035	0215	0036	0237	
3) CABIN 3	0030	0255	0030	0250	0030	0245	0025	0240	0030	0307	
4) COMCEN	0125	0420	0120	0410	0120	0405	0130	0410	0026	0333	
5) GANTRY 2 LOBBY	0045	0505	0035	0445	0035	0440	0035	0445	0037	04.10	
6) COMMON ROOM	0050	0555	0045	0530	0045	0525	0045	0530	0045	04.55	
7) COMCEN R	0055	0650	0100	0630	0100	0625	0020	0550	0020	05.15	
8) CABIN 3	0115	0805	0100	0730	0100	0725	0115?	0705	0053	0608	
9) CABIN 1	0010	0815	0010	0740	0010	0735	0010	0715	0010 0007	0618 0625	
10) GYM	0135	0950	0135	0915	0130	0905	0140	0855	OUT →		
11) CABIN 1	0055	1045	0115	1030	0125	1030	0110	1005	0040	0705	
12) CABIN CORRIDOR	0035	1120	0030	1100	0030	1100	0030	1035	0036	0741	
13) CABIN 1	0035	1155	0035	1135	0040	1140	0045	1120	0048	0829	
14) CABIN 3	0105	1300	0140	1315	0135	1315	0135	1255	0131	1001	
15) COMCEN	0045	1345	0045	1400	0055	1410	0120	1415	0125	1126	
16) CABIN 1	0040	1425	0040	1440	0040	1450	0100	1515	0102	1228	
END PART ONE	0005	1430	0005	1445	0005	1455	0005	1520	0003	12.31	
	PT1	1430	PT1	1445	PT1	1455	Part 1	1520	Part 1	1231	
	PT2	1027	PT2	1117	PT2	1100	Part 2	1110	Part 2	1154	
24'57	TOTAL	[illegible]	TOTAL	[illegible]	TOTAL	[illegible]	TOTAL	[illegible]	TOTAL	[illegible]	

Fig. 18. The PA notes the running time of each scene – from the first rehearsal through to the producer's Run, the studio, and the edit.

MEMORANDUM

from J.H.Parker.

to H.Foster,S.Duckett,Sound Dubbing.

date 20/12/90

JUPITER MOON DUBBING NOTES EPISODES 136-138.

Episode 136.

Sc 5 Door open.

Sc 8 Door open and close.

Sc 10 Lift arrive,stop and depart.

Sc 16 Door open and close.

Sc 18 Door open and close.

Sc 20 Composed of different passes and pickups.
Start of sequence Roll 203/28-19
WT trolley Roll 203/44-16
WT crockery breaking Roll 203/44-38

Sc 22 Composed of different passes and pickups.
Start of sequence Roll 203/37-48

Sc 26 Doors open and close.

Sc 29A Door open and close X 2.

Sc 31 Door open and close X 2.
Door buzz on light cue.
WT Daniel´s "Lights." Roll 204/45-04

Episode 137.

Sc 1 Door open and close.
Music "Africa".

Sc 2 Add FX of two cups of coffee being poured.

Sc 3 Door open and close.
Music "Africa".

Sc 10 Lift arrive.

(Continued)

Fig. 19. After the studio the sound effects are dubbed onto the tape.

PROGRAMME AS COMPLETED FORM PAGE 1 (of 12)

TRANSMISSION INFORMATION

BSB

IF PROGRAMME IS DELIVERED ON DAY OF TRANSMISSION **PLEASE**
FAX TOP SHEET (THIS PAGE (1)) TO PRESENTATION DEPT. FAX. NO.: 627 6565
FAX PAGES 2 AND 3 (COMMERCIAL REFERENCES TO AIR TIME SALES Fax. NO.: 627 6256
HARD COPY OF PAGES 1-12 TO PROGRAMME SERVICES DEPT. FAX NO.: 627 6556

PROGRAMME TITLE: JUPITER MOON.
BSB PROG. NO: 00012580
SERIES TITLE: JUPITER MOON EP 136 OF
FIRST TX DATE/TIME: CHANNEL:
IS PROGRAMME CONTINUOUS OR DISCONTINOUS? DISCONTINUOUS
ARE THERE END/BEGINNING OF PART CAPTIONS? YES
PLEASE INDICATE BELOW ACTUAL OR ADVISORY BREAK POINTS.
Pt 1. TC IN: 00:03:00:00 TC OUT: 00:14:13:06 DURATION: 11':13"
CUE IN:
CUE OUT:
Pt 2. TC IN: 00:16:00:00 TC OUT: 00:28:51:00 DURATION: 12':51
CUE IN:
CUE OUT:
Pt 3. TC IN: : : : TC OUT: : : : TOTAL DURATION: 24':04"
CUE IN:
CUE OUT:
(PLEASE CONTINUE MORE PARTS ON SEPARATE SHEET)
TOTAL PROGRAMME DURATION (min:sec): 24:04.
FIRST END CREDIT: TIMOTHY SHAW (ANDREW READ) AT TC: 00:28:02:15
LAST END CREDIT: PRIMETIME ANDROMEDA AT TC: 00:28:51:00
DOES PROG CONTINUE AFTER LAST END CREDIT? NO
ATTACH ANY CONTACT NUMBERS OR ADDRESSES MENTIONED IN PROGRAMME. PLEASE ADVISE OF ANY FACTORS AFFECTING TRANSMISSION OF PROG., (eg. Mute sections, Periods of black, Contrived breakdowns, Deliberate distortion of sound or vision)

PRODUCTION COMPANY: TEL:
ADDRESS: FAX:

PRODUCER/DIRECTOR HOME TEL:
ADDRESS:

PRODUCTION COMPANY'S TAPE NO: 719SP30

PLEASE RETURN ALL THESE COPIES TO B.S.B., THE MARCOPOLO BUILDING, QUEENSTOWN ROAD, LONDON SW8 4NQ.

Fig. 20. Transmission details are sent to the broadcasting station.

12

The Difficult Markets

WHICH ARE THE MOST DIFFICULT MARKETS?

The hardest markets for new writers to break into are:

- single plays
- serials
- adaptations.

SINGLE PLAYS

These are the prestige dramas that aspire to say something significant about the world in which we live. Through the single television play some of the best writers in Britain have been discovered and nurtured. Playwrights like David Edgar, David Hare, David Rudkin (David is clearly a helpful name in television drama) have written some of their most important work for the single television play slot.

Today, sadly, few writers are discovered and nurtured, and this has become one of the most difficult slots for the beginner. There are two reasons for this. Firstly, ITV has moved more and more to long-running series dramas that can build a mass audience and sell overseas. Secondly, the cost of making the single play has risen sharply because of the expectations of viewers.

What viewers look for

When Sydney Newman was producing *Armchair Theatre* on ITV the single drama was both popular viewing and cheap to make. Writers nurtured on the theatrical tradition wrote intelligent plays in which the action was contained in one or two studio sets, and which had few characters.

Today viewers expect more. They expect single plays to be shot on film, they expect gloss and colour and excitement on the screen, they expect to be visually as well as mentally entertained. The cost of single-play drama shot on film can now be well over a million pounds per hour. This is the most expensive television there is.

The BBC and Channel 4 still make single plays of the highest quality. Single plays are still, occasionally, made on ITV. But there are fewer slots than in the past, and it is increasingly rare for these precious, prestigious, incredibly expensive dramas to be given over to a new writer.

Single plays are normally written by:

- television writers with a track record; a writer puts forward an idea to a producer he knows, and is then commissioned to write a script

- writers from other media – journalism, literature – who already have a high (or at least interesting) reputation.

Even among prestigious writers more scripts are commissioned (such is the power of a good lunch and a persuasive top literary agent in a Charlotte Street restaurant) than there are slots available. When a new writer sends in an unsolicited script, therefore, he is likely to be competing for the sole remaining slot of the year against a script by an established writer that has already cost the BBC or Channel 4 several thousands of pounds.

Should a new writer bother writing a one-off play?

The answer is most definitely YES – and for the following reasons:

- In the one-off 60-minute or 90-minute play you are creating your own world, with your own characters, in your own style. Your writing is likely to be at its best and its most convincing. As was said in **How to succeed** on page 14, a single play of your own devising is your *curriculum vitae* – your claim to be taken seriously.

- There is the possibility that you will achieve something wonderful, and that your play will be read by a producer who likes it and has the opportunity to put it on. There is also the possibility that your play will be read and remembered later.

  It does happen. A completely unknown writer sent a 90-minute film script to BBC Pebble Mill. It was liked by a script editor who pushed it for production, but without success. Months later a production collapsed and there was a search for a replacement.

The unknown writer – who had given up hope – received a phone call to say that her play would start pre-production the following week, with Jane Lapotaire in the lead role.

- There is a good chance that if your play shows genuine talent you will be considered as a writer for another slot. Many writers on soap operas and series dramas first attracted attention to their skills by submitting single plays.

Step by step for the new writer

1. Unless you have a story that needs 90 minutes, write for a 60-minute slot. There are more of these available than 75- or 90-minute slots.

2. On no account write for longer than 90 minutes.

3. Write a script that shows us a genuinely fresh, original aspect of contemporary life. It might be family drama, or comedy drama, or gritty social drama – but you need to bring to it a new slant, a new voice.

4. For Channel 4, check the online guide for producers (*www.channel4.co.uk*) to see if particular types of drama are in demand.

5. Do not write period drama, because it is very expensive and single plays almost always concern themselves with life today.

6. If you have specialist knowledge use it. Try to take us into a world that you know better than anyone else. If you have given birth to a baby and spent a year under the Pacific in a nuclear submarine you have at least two experiences that put you one up on the majority of TV dramatists.

7. Write for a reasonably small cast (i.e. don't demand hundreds of participating extras) and avoid elaborate and expensive set-ups (i.e. don't demand that jumbo jets crash into the Dome or that filming takes place at a hot air balloon rally at the South Pole) because producers often look for low-cost dramas (in BBC terms £600,000 an hour rather than £1,200,000) to compensate for the high-budget plays to which they have previously committed themselves.

8. Write for film, with outside locations. Few single dramas are now shot in the studio.

9. Try to think of interesting but low-cost locations: fairgrounds give colour and visual interest, and fairgrounds are not too difficult for the production to find. Canal barges, the seaside, a hot air balloon rally that *isn't* at the South Pole – these are locations that get us out and about without costing the production a fortune. Try to think of locations that are cheap but different!

> Whether in subject matter or treatment, contemporary is the watchword.
>
> (BBC 1 Drama Department)

SERIALS

A serial tells an ongoing story and has a set number of episodes. Often serials are in four parts, or six parts, but this is a matter of fashion and changes year by year. Serials include original dramas and adaptations of popular novels and classics.

There have traditionally been few opportunities here for the new writer. A drama department might make three or four serials a year, and will have a huge choice of materials and writers to select from. If it is rare for television to commission a new writer for a one-off play, it is almost unheard of to commission four or six hours of drama from somebody with no track record. BBC1 says it is looking for 'signature writers' which is another way of saying big names.

But television is constantly changing, and if you have a strong idea for a serial – say a thriller, or comedy drama in four or six episodes – then you should go for it. Channel 4 has plans for innovative low-cost drama, and BBC 2 is actively looking for new ideas for late night serials that can be 30-minute, 40-minute or 50-minute in duration. There must be opportunities here for the new writer.

Step by step for the new writer

1. Write an opening episode and a synopsis of the other episodes. Each synopsis should be around three or four pages long (reasonably spaced out and easy to read). Don't break your synopses down into scenes but tell the broad sweep of the story,

showing that each episode has an exciting opening, strong development, and climax.

2. Your best chance is to write for a low-budget slot – in television terms this means under £400,000 an episode, and both Channel 4 and BBC 2 would be very, very happy if a strong well-scripted story was offered to them for £100,000 an episode. BBC 2 says hopefully that its late night slot has potential for those who embrace 'new technology and/or ways of working'. From a writer's point of view: make it low cost with no car chases and few locations.

3. As with the one-off single drama, give us something fresh and original. Script editors yearn for something exciting, that hasn't been done before.

ADAPTATIONS

Whether it be classic period adaptations like *Wives and Daughters* or *Emma,* or a modern novel like *The History Man*, the television company embarking on a multi-million pound project is going to look for a writer of experience to adapt the original material. This is probably the most difficult market to get into.

Like most writers, though, you probably have a favourite book (let us call it *Pigs Might Fly*) which you believe would make a terrific television serial. It is just possible that you could offer your adaptation at exactly the right time to a producer who a) is also passionately fond of *Pigs Might Fly*, b) thinks you have done a terrific adaptation and c) has the muscle to get both the book and you accepted by the network scheduler.

In the case of classic novels, you should write a synopsis of the dramatic ground you would cover in each episode, and then write the first episode as an example of your work.

With modern novels, it is a more interesting situation. The work is in copyright, and the television rights could easily have been sold elsewhere. You might spend weeks toiling on an adaptation only to find that another writer is doing the same – but under commission from a television company that has taken out an option on the book.

If you believe your skills lie in the field of adaptation do not be put off trying, but check the following before you start.

- Has the novel been done on television before, and if so how long ago was it? Generally speaking television does not worry about things previously done in black and white.

- Are the television rights in the work available? The publisher will give you the name of the writer's agent, who will have this information.

- If the rights are available, will the writer agree to you adapting their work? Many writers, sensibly, are careful about who they allow to adapt their novels.

If the rights are available, and the writer has no objection to you as adaptor, all you have to do is find a television company interested in putting it on.

Can I acquire rights in a book myself?

Yes, of course – again if the writer is willing to give you an option. Independent producers often take out options on books and then try to sell the idea to a television company.

In the general run of things an option on a book is not expensive. You can secure an option for twelve months for a few hundred pounds. This gives you the exclusive right to make a television programme out of the book during the period of the option. As you would expect, to option a bestseller or a book by a very successful author will be much more expensive.

Of course you might be lucky enough to buy the rights in a book just before it becomes an international bestseller – and then have the satisfaction of having the BBC, ITV and Channel 4 desperate to get hold of it, and happy to commission you as the adaptor. Everybody can dream . . .

> BBC 2 drama is about making a statement, creating landmarks, and adding colour and diversity to the schedule.
>
> (BBC Commissioning Guide)

13

Programmes Looking for Writers

WHICH ARE THE BEST PROGRAMMES TO TRY?

The television slots that offer the most opportunity to new writers are:

- series dramas
- short plays
- children's drama
- situation comedy.

(Soap operas are covered separately in the next chapter.)

SERIES DRAMAS

Series dramas generally run for an hour, and there are a lot of them on television. In a series we have an established situation and established central characters, but each week we have a new story that also brings in its own characters.

A series will sometimes have only six or seven episodes, but more often it will have a magnificent 13, and will run for a quarter of the year.

Programme schedulers love series dramas because they build up an audience week by week. New writers ought to love them because of the opportunity they present.

How to write for a series

In its first run a series might have been written by a picked team of three or four writers (usually including the series devisor), but when a further series is planned the script editors instantly start to look around for fresh blood. Thirteen scripts might not seem too difficult to find, but to get them 40 or 50 storylines might be considered, and many of those will be put through two or three drafts. Then, perhaps 15 scripts will be commissioned – and when the first five come in and are hopeless the editor will panic and commission a whole lot more.

This may seem profligate, as fees can be over £6,000 for a 60-minute slot and the first half payment (50 per cent up front) will be paid whether the script is accepted or not. Consider, though, that each programme is going to cost up to a million pounds to make, and that the BBC or ITV scheduler will rely on it to deliver an audience of 9 to 12 million contented viewers who will not only enjoy this episode, but turn on again the following week.

With so much at stake it is well worth commissioning three or even four scripts in order to get one that is good.

A 13-part series might therefore provide gainful employment to more than 25 writers. And still, at the end of the day, weak scripts will be accepted and go into production with the producers and script editor blindly relying on production values, in other words excitement on screen and glitzy casting – 'if in doubt cast up' – to save the day.

The writer shortage

The shortage of good writers in this area is acute. Script editors are often in despair, wondering where to turn next. All too often the choice is between the script editor's chum who works in the fringe theatre and rather despises television, or the weary old hack who has been churning them out since *Z Cars* and the first series of *Howard's Way*. When a new writer with sparkle, imagination and technical skill comes along he is sobbed over, cosseted, commissioned for new episodes and taken out for extravagant lunches. This could be you.

Step by step for the new writer

Select the series you would most like to write for.

1. In doing this, consider both your tastes in drama and any specialist knowledge you might have. *London's Burning* will look favourably on a promising writer who has been a fireman; *Casualty* will be interested in a script from a trained midwife.

2. Ideally, make your approach when the series is being transmitted and is getting a good audience response. This is often the time a decision on a further series is made.

3. Phone the production company that makes the programme and ask if a further series is planned.

4. Attempt to speak directly to the script editor or producer, and ask if they are willing to read an example of your work.

5. If they say 'yes' send them a copy of an original play you have written.

6. If you cannot speak directly to them, find out their names so that you can write to them personally.

7. Send an example of your writing. Say you would like the opportunity to submit a storyline. Ask if there will be changes to the basic format in the new series, i.e. are major characters being written-out, is the location changing? Ask for a copy of any new format notes for writers.

You can try to get new format notes during your first phone call, but the production office is unlikely to send out details of format changes to somebody who has phoned out of the blue and has not written for television before.

If the script editor is looking for new writers, though, and likes the writing sample you have sent, then she will encourage you to submit a storyline and will give you the same format notes that are being sent to experienced writers.

Common queries

Does it matter what sort of writing sample I send?
Yes. If you are hoping to write for *Heartbeat* it is not helpful to send a gritty play about urban deprivation in Brixton. The script editor is trying to judge whether your talents for characterisation, dialogue and plotting would make you suitable for the series she is editing. Don't make life difficult for her.

Should I send an episode of the series I want to write for?
No. Editors are not impressed by pale imitations of what you are seeing on the screen, and you do not have the current information regarding format. Editors want an example of what you, the writer, do best on your own initiative: your own characters, dialogue and style.

Should I send in lots of ideas for the series to show my ability and interest?
Again you do not have the relevant format information, and editors are not really interested in storyline ideas until they know you have the ability to write. That said, if you put forward a first-class storyline, well structured and succinctly told, so gripping that the

editor can't put it down – then you are likely to get an interested response.

How do I write a storyline?
You have to put forward, in a clear, easy to understand manner, the story you are proposing. You have to make it exciting to the reader. You have to show that your drama opens in an interesting way, sustains itself, and has a good ending. It does not matter if your storyline is one page or six pages long, if what you write does the job. But the following guidelines might be useful to the beginner.

- Give an interesting summary of your story or stories: 'Wealthy Sir Solomon Featherstone leaves £50,000 in his will so that his friends can enjoy the party of a lifetime. And so they do – until a group of shaken guests swear they saw Sir Solomon himself dancing at the disco. Det Insp Friday disinters the coffin – and uncovers more than he expects'.

- For a 50-minute series episode an editor will normally expect a three- or four-page storyline. (Between 500 and 1,200 words.)

- If you are writing for ITV the editor will look for strong endings to part one and part two – preferably edge-of-seat endings that keep viewers interested, and stop them from slipping away to other channels during the adverts.

- If the storyline has two or three strands – perhaps a main story, a secondary story and a comic sub-story – the editor will look to see how skilfully stories develop and intertwine, and how you propose to contrast quiet moments in one story with action in another (see Chapter 4).

- Take care not to get bogged down in detail – 'He says to her, then she goes out and he turns to somebody else and says...' – but stick to the main story developments. You are writing a synopsis not a blow-by-blow account.

SHORT PLAYS OR 'SHORTS'

There was a time when 30-minute series strands were devoted to the search for new writers – *Second City First* for example, which was produced in the studio at BBC Pebble Mill and introduced new writers and new directors through simple plays with one or two sets, a small cast, small budget and small, late night audiences.

The fashion now is for even shorter plays – usually about ten minutes long, depending on the BBC or Channel 4 slot – which are often filmed on location. *He Plays She Plays* and *Brief Encounters* are two of the recent strands on Channel 4. Some series have an individual character, perhaps specialising in zany and off-beat stories, or stories about contemporary male–female relationships. Other series take a joy in offering something totally different every week. The types of story will generally reflect the tastes of the producer.

Some of these slots prefer to make short dramas by established writers, but others have a deliberate policy of encouraging new talent.

One difficulty is also an opportunity. Many of the slots – pioneered by Anglia's *First Take* and *10x10* by BBC Bristol – are primarily aimed at encouraging new directors rather than new writers. It is the would-be director, often from film school, who approaches the television company with a show-reel of their work and a script. But where do the directors get their scripts from? They have no money to buy scripts, and no access to professional writers. If you have an idea for a film it is worth ringing film schools to see if there are talented unknown directors desperately seeking talented unknown writers. It is also worth ringing regional arts associations, who bring together local writers and directors and occasionally help with co-funding (the Arts Council and South East Arts have both co-funded a *10x10*).

This is a very competitive area – BBC Bristol gets 600 applicants for 10 slots – but at least it is primarily aimed at new talent.

Step by step for the new writer

1. Watch each series and note the one you enjoy the most, and the name of the producer or script editor.

2. Phone and ask if another series is being produced. Ask if you can submit a script. Ask if the programme works in conjunction with any particular film schools or arts funding bodies.

3. Additional information on Channel 4 can be found in *Writing Proposals to Channel Four* obtainable from Channel 4, 124 Horseferry Road, London SW1P 2TX. Tel: (020) 7396 4444 or look on the website at *www.channel4.co.uk*

4. Approach film schools and/or local arts associations to say that

you are interested in writing a script for a new director.

5. If the television production office is non-committal, and the film schools not wildly enthusiastic, write a script anyway. This is only a ten-minute drama and you can afford to make the effort.
6. Before writing, note the number of locations normally used, and the average number of scenes (interior and exterior) and the number of cast.
7. Remember that 'shorts' are low budget – this means perhaps £15,000 to £25,000 – so the fewer actors you use the better. Also remember that 'shorts' are primarily aimed at developing director skills. Your story must have the potential to be visually interesting.
8. Let all the above information sink into your subconscious, do not fret over it, do not try to produce a copy of what has gone before – just bear the parameters in mind, and proceed to write a ten-minute script that is original and your own.
9. Send it to the producer or editor, by name, with a simple covering letter (see page 137) or to a film school or arts association drama officer saying that you would like to work with a trainee director.

> I regard myself as a storyteller, a narrative playwright, so a successful series episode, to me, is one in which I have managed to write my own original play within the framework of the series, without anyone noticing.
>
> (N. J. Crisp, writer)

CHILDREN'S DRAMA

The requirement for children's drama is exactly the same as for any other kind of drama, be it one-off plays (of which very few are made) or series and serials (of which there are a lot). There is always a demand for good contemporary ideas – programmes like *Byker Grove* and the teenage soap *Hollyoaks*. Children's drama is low budget, so historical dramas are more difficult to sell than contemporary themes. (Classical adaptations often have period settings, but in this area experienced writers are always used.) Producers say they do not want clichéd situations – animals that can talk, time travel – but it is noticeable that programmes are still being made using these themes. Comedy or fantasy is wanted for the younger age groups. Prominent drama slots are:

- 15-minute drama at 4.15pm aimed at 6–8 year olds.
- 30-minute drama (original or adaptations) at 4.30pm aimed at the 7–9 year olds.
- 30-minute drama (original or adaptations) at 5.00pm aimed at the 10–12 year olds.

Children's programming guidelines

When writing for children certain guidelines have to be observed – which essentially means being careful with the following:

1. Situations arising from adoption, desertion, cruelty in the home, which could threaten a child's emotional security.
2. Portrayal of injury or disablement, or embarrassing personal disabilities like stuttering.
3. The use of weapons or poisons to cause injury or death.
4. Joke stunts that could be copied with disastrous results – stretching wire across a path, for example, to dismount a cyclist.
5. Heroes and heroines who smoke and drink alcohol.
6. The infliction of pain or humiliation on others. Suffering of children or animals.

SITUATION COMEDIES

Everybody is looking for comedy scriptwriters. They are the best paid writers, they are the most in demand – and they suffer the most rejection. Every year the BBC, ITV and Channel 4 produce their crop of new situation comedies (often from new writers) and every year the critics and viewers are mercilessly dismissive. For every *Birds of a Feather* there are a clutch of sitcoms that bite the dust, desperately unfunny, mourned only by the sad writer who worked so hard at the jokes and the poor actors who had to play them.

It is because comedy is so difficult to judge that both the BBC and ITV are prepared to spend large sums of money making pilot programmes of sitcoms, and why there are now several comedy workshops where scripts – often by new writers – can be tried out on live audiences.

What programme makers say they want

- Comedies that are 'intelligent, character-based, and up-market'. (ITV)
- Stories that are unpredictable with twists to keep an audience guessing.
- Comedies which 'draw their strength from realistic and relevant situations and characters'. (BBC 1)
- Comedies that have a 'simple and funny high-concept premise which immediately suggests comic possibilities'. (BBC Comedy Script Unit)
- Comedies that will attract a younger audience and appeal to younger women. (BBC 2)

In all cases, these ideas must have the potential to generate and support future storylines.

What programme makers say they don't want

- Familiar themes: flat-sharing, the chap who's won the pools, mothers-in-law situation, grandads who come to stay and won't go home.
- Contrived situations and elaborate contrivances to keep the characters together.
- 'Down-market, class-ridden comedies'. (ITV)
- Comedies that rely on 'strings of gags and funny lines'. (BBC) In other words the old time, third-rate ITV sitcom with artificial situations and farcical stories.
- Comedies that need expensive filming. Almost all situation comedy is studio-based, sometimes with a small amount of OB.

Step by step for the new writer

1. Use the Internet to access advice on who is currently seeking scripts. Look at the BBC's Comedy Zone, and at sites like *Situations Vacant* for companies willing to pilot new ideas (see Chapter 18, page 169).

2. Write a brief outline of your idea, its premise, and your main characters. First try to sum up the idea in around 25 words (e.g. A sleepy, old-fashioned rural community suddenly finds its new vicar is a bubbly, enthusiastic, female who is determined to make things happen!). Your entire proposal should not be more than two pages long (well presented without too much dense writing) because the script reader will have already assessed several other proposals before reaching yours, and she will need all the mental assistance you can give her.

3. Write the brief plot outline for the first two or three episodes (keeping each outline as short as possible), then write a full script for the episode that follows.

4. Send your script and outline to independent production companies before going directly to the BBC. If the BBC has turned your script down the independents will not be interested – but if an independent turns you down there half a dozen others that you can try, and an independent who likes your idea can offer it to the BBC, ITV, Channel 4, Channel 5 (which says it wants to commission more drama and comedy programmes) and Sky (which says the same, though perhaps with less conviction).

5. Of the main production companies, Hat Trick Productions, Channel X Communications, LWT, and Noel Gay Television say they will look at unsolicited scripts, Tiger Aspect will look at unsolicited proposals, and Carlton will only look at scripts from experienced writers and agents. (For details of these and other production companies see Chapter 19.)

6. Send your script and outline to at least two companies at the same time. If you go round the independents one by one you could be a hundred and receive your telegram from the Queen before you get the final rejection letter. If one company takes you up, you can tell the others that your work is no longer available.

7. The BBC Comedy Script Unit (see Chapter 19) will give you a script reader's assessment even if it rejects your script. (It will not, however, read it again after you have rewritten it.) If the initial assessment is promising you will be asked to a meeting with a script editor, so that your script or idea can be developed.

8. Don't give up on a script too soon. Comedy is so individual that you work could be rejected by half a dozen producers – and then taken up with enthusiasm by the next. At the same time, if several producers give a very clear and consistent reason for rejection ('Dear Sitcom Writer, you may not have noticed but there has already been a comedy series about a jolly lady vicar in a rural community...') then they are probably telling you something that you ought to know.

> If you have never written a sitcom before, it might help you to tape episodes of your favourite series and watch them a few times, noting the scene structure, story development, frequency of laughs and the balance of verbal and visual jokes.
> (Robin Kelly)
>
> Take your characters up a tree and then lob rocks at them.
> (Caryn Mandabach, producer *3rd Rock from the Sun*)

14

Soap Operas

A LARGE AND GROWING MARKET

Many new writers get their first chance in television by writing for the soap operas. Many stay in the world of 'soaps' and become seriously well-off, particularly if they are writing programmes with automatic repeats like *Coronation Street* and *Eastenders* (these are the two programmes, naturally enough, most difficult to get on to). Soap operas do not always succeed – *Jupiter Moon* ended when Sky Television took over BSB, *Families* and *Eldorado* were costly mistakes – but when they are established they can go on for a very long time, and provide steady long-term work for writers. New soaps in recent years have included Channel 5's *Family Affairs* (which has taken on several young writers completely new to television) and Channel 4's *Hollyoaks*.

Some soap operas bring in extra money from overseas sales. *Jupiter Moon* can be seen on cable and satellite in the USA, and the Scottish Television soap *Take the High Road* was, for some reason, so popular in Sri Lanka that at one time it filled the Saturday evening prime-time slot.

Soap operas represent a huge market. Even the established soaps are using more writers, as they expand to make more programmes. At any given moment half-a-dozen script editors will be actively on the look-out for new writing talent.

To write for a soap opera you need to:

- take a lively interest in the domestic drama of everyday life
- respect popular drama and regard it as worthwhile and important
- have the ability to work with other writers, and to help formulate stories in storyline meetings

STORY SO FAR

Pot-bellied, whisky-pickled union shop convenor BILL HODDER is all set for tomorrow's freebie visit to a Bayonne engineering works.

In the meantime he and wife LIZ have been promised a wedding-anniversary outing by son CLIVE.

CLIVE, though, has forgotten his filial duties and fixed a date with SANDRA BREWSTER.

JOHN SCHOFIELD, project engineer at Alfred Holt, is worried by a sudden, mystifying cut in development funds.

GILLIAN BREWSTER, 13, is within an ace of getting her own pony.

SANDRA BREWSTER is having a terrible time. Last week she was told she wasn't good enough for the shorthand/typing job her father FRANK got for her.

At the end of the last episode her father found out.

We last saw her sitting, anguished, on her bed, while FRANK stormed up the stairs....

Fig. 21. A serial drama script editor will write either a 'Story So Far' or an episode synopsis to accompany each script.

1. INT. HALLWAY. BREWSTERS. DAY (From Episode 11)

Opening theme music as we see FRANK turn at the bottom of the stairs and start to climb them, a grim, set look on his face.

FRANK
Sandra! Sandra!

2. INT. SANDRA'S BEDROOM. DAY (From Episode 11)

17 year-old SANDRA sits hunched up on her bed. Hearing her father's voice she looks in distress towards the door. She's for it now!

CUT TO:

OPENING TITLES

3. SANDRA'S BEDROOM. DAY

FADE IN on FRANK pacing up and down, exercising his powers of mental creativity. SANDRA still sits hunched up on the bed, but is now snivelling over a shorthand pad.

FRANK
And in conclusion I would like to express my gratitude for the esteemed honour---

SANDRA
We haven't done esteemed!

FRANK
The esteemed honour of the valued custom you have so kindly given to us---

SANDRA
I've never had esteemed said to me in me life---

FRANK
So kindly given to us and I confirm delivery of same by the fourteenth ult.

Fig. 22. A writer picks up the story from a previous episode – in this case there is a reprise of the final scene of the previous programme.

- be able to write imaginative, lively scripts within the restrictions of length, sets, locations and cast that are imposed
- thoroughly understand the nature of long-running serial drama – the 'soap formula'.

THE SOAP FORMULA

> I remember, in those early days, likening the *Crossroads* cast to birds in a nest, with their beaks wide open, yelling for 'More plot, more dialogue, more problems, more solutions...'
>
> (Reg Watson, producer of *Crossroads* and *Neighbours*)

Soap operas use up a ferocious amount of dramatic material. There are always at least three running stories that are not interconnected, and once those stories are exhausted new ones involving different characters must take their place.

The vital part of the formula is that we must be able to go, effortlessly, into the homes of our characters for an inexhaustible supply of domestic dramas.

There might be a big story of love and passion at Domicile A, a running tale of ambition and money at Domicile B, and a running comedy theme at Domicile C. It is important that these dramas need only relate to each other (be it in the pub, shop, factory) when we want them to.

The simpler the structure and more ordinary the location the better. The identity of a soap opera is created by its characterisation, plotting and view of life, not by any originality or novelty in format.

SOAP OPERA STORIES

Soap operas are popular dramas, aimed at every age and class. They have inherited the mantle of the minstrel and the teller of folk tales, the mantle worn by Trollope and Dickens and a host of less talented but equally prolific writers. At their worst (and there is a lot of their worst) they are bland and repetitious; at their best they are as good as any drama on television.

Opinion polls have told us what viewers look for.

- Different generations of people – babies and teenagers, adults and senior citizens.

- Love affairs, engagements, marriages, divorces, and all the complications resulting from male–female relationships.
- Young people and young people's problems – teenage 'going off the rails', school activities.
- Young couples living together. Homebuilding, pregnancy, unemployment.
- Humour.
- Community gossip, scandal, intrigue and curiosity.
- Larger-than-life characters – rogues, tarts, stirrers, snobs, gossips... people that ordinary folk can identify with.

SCRIPTS AND WRITERS

If you have six writers on your team, then at any given moment one of them will be on the way out. A writer might be going abroad for a few months, or want to take time off to write a novel, or might simply want to get off the soap opera treadmill. Then again the writer might not know he is on the way out, that sadly his time will be up just as soon as the script editor can find a replacement.

Many writers are kept on the team long after the producer, editor and cast have been sent screaming mad by boring, empty dialogue, pathetic characterisation, repetitive and unimaginative scenes. They are kept on – often to their own surprise – because at the end of the day they can be relied on to deliver a script that:

- is the right length with a commercial break reasonably near the middle
- has the right number of characters
- uses the right sets with the right amount of OB
- covers the stories that the storyline says it should cover
- does not steal stories the storyline has allocated to the next writer.

The script editor opens the tired writer's script with a sinking heart, knowing she is going to have to stay up half the night trying to inject a modicum of sparkle and believability into the dialogue – but also knowing that on a primitive, basic level the script will work. It won't have to be binned. It will be pretty awful, but the cast will act their little socks off and it will get by.

And in the meantime, the search for a replacement writer will continue.

Step by step for the new writer

The first thing you must do is to choose your soap opera.

1. Identify the soap opera that you, as a viewer, most enjoy watching.

Among the urban TV soaps *Coronation Street* and *Eastenders* are identical in structure (working-class homes focusing on a pub; one in its time had a factory making jeans and the other a street market selling them), but vastly different in style. *Coronation Street* draws strength from Northern values and Northern humour, and often gives us a laugh. *Eastenders* reflects – indeed, sometimes seems to prey on – a glum world where life is gritty and grim. *Emmerdale* has its own characteristics, and they are far from being the characteristics of *Brookside*. There was once a writer who, using two names, was on the team of both *Coronation Street* and *Crossroads*, but generally speaking writers are faithful to one programme because their view of life and writing style suits only one programme.

2. Identify the programme you are best qualified to write for.

If you grew up on a farm in Yorkshire, trained as a vet, regard all southerners as effete, and would rather go down a coal mine than watch dramas about lesbians and Aids victims, then you are more likely to find a welcome on *Emmerdale* than *Eastenders*.

3. Have a sample of work to show.

Evidence of your ability is vital. Editors want to see how you handle characters, plots and above all dialogue. In the first instance editors usually prefer to see a single play you have written and do *not* want to see your attempt at writing their soap opera.

Make sure your writing sample is something that will help the script editor to assess your suitability – in other words contemporary drama based on dialogue and character rather than action.

4. Find out the name of the script editor, either by watching the credits or by phoning the production office.

5. If you do phone the production office ask if the programme has its own system of assessing new writers – trial scripts, perhaps, or new writers' seminars.

6. Send your sample script with a short covering letter.

If there is something in your background you think might be useful (you've been a social worker/vet; you're the Director of Programme's mistress/boyfriend), say so. Otherwise the letter should be short and to the point, as in the example shown in Figure 23.

7. Make sure you know the programme thoroughly.

If the script editor likes your original script she will either write encouraging you to submit a trial sample script (unpaid!), or she will speak to you on the phone (curious to know more about you) or invite you in to talk.

If you are lucky she will just have had one writer bundled into a drying-out clinic, another run off to Latin America, and been forced by the producer to sack another. If you are unlucky the programme will have recently received three or four scripts from very promising new writers, and not be looking for more.

Either way, you have to be ready. You have to know about the programme – the characters, the locations, the stories in recent episodes. You must be able to say, instantly, what the current three running stories are. You must be able to say which characters you think are being written well for, and which are not. You must be able to project enthusiasm and have sensible, realistic ideas.

If you are encouraged to write a sample script, ask for a couple of back scripts, preferably by different writers, and any writers' guidance notes that exist.

8. Do not copy the style of other writers.

Other writers' scripts, and episodes you have taped and studied, will give you a feel for the programme. But the script editor is not looking for a pale imitation of the past. She is looking for dialogue that is new and fresh; characters that ring true and honest, but are illuminated in a brighter, more vivid, more believable way; stories that are developed with verve and energy.

What next?

Assume your sample script was brilliant and you have been commissioned to write an episode. The script editor will not object to being sent flowers at this point. Even feminists like flowers. You

Ms Zia Wanascript
'Coronenders'
Friendly Television Company,
Moneygalore Road
London 1AA 6BQ

9 June 200X

Dear Zia Wanascript

I am interested in writing for Coronenders and enclose as an example of my work a 60-minute television play called 'Promise'.

I would be happy to write a sample script for Coronenders if you think this would be worthwhile.

If so, I would be grateful for any guidance notes for writers that you might have.

(or)

I understand that you occasionally hold seminars for new writers. I would be grateful for the chance to attend one of these.

I hope you enjoy reading 'Promise'.

Your sincerely

Julian Goodwriter

Fig. 23. How to write a covering letter for a sample script.

will be asked to the studio, shown round the set, lunched in the canteen. You are a professional writer. Congratulations! You now have your first **scriptmeeting** to face.

How soap operas are written

Every soap opera varies slightly in its script production methods. Some programmes (like *Eastenders*) try to give scriptwriters an element of creative freedom, other soaps are very much a production line, with every scene, and the reaction of every character to every event, mapped out by storyliners. What follows is a typical fortnight on one of the more chaotic soaps.

Scriptmeeting

Up to a dozen writers meet for a day with the producer, two script editors and storyliners. They already have a long-term storyline. On this occasion they thrash out the stories for a fortnight of episodes. At this point the writers do not know which episode they will write – or even if they will write at all. They are expected to contribute ideas for all the episodes. If they do not show keenness and enthusiasm, they might not be commissioned to write at all.

Scripts commissioned

The storyliners (who are almost always young, stressed-out, would-be writers themselves) work feverishly to prepare a storyline for each episode, showing commercial breaks and episode cliffhangers. Writers are phoned and offered an episode. They are told the schedule this time is very tight, and that they can only have four days to write their script.

Storyline approved

There is a delay while producers and executive producers read the storylines and demand changes. Writers are phoned and told that their storylines are going to be late, but will be faxed or e-mailed to them. They ask if they can have a later delivery time. They are told no they can't.

Episodes written

The storylines reach the writers. They start work. After several hours they are phoned again and told that their storyline has to be changed because of story objections from the channel head of drama. Writers again ask if they can have a later delivery date. Again they are told no they can't.

Scripts back

The scripts come in, often by e-mail, and are edited by the script editors. Rewrites might be demanded by phone or fax, and will need to be completed within a matter of hours. The scripts go to the producer, then to the script typist, and then into production.

The storyliners are already preparing for the next scriptmeeting...

Six weeks or so later

The episodes are made, both in the studio and on location. On five-days-a-week soaps there is little or no rehearsal. On the more leisurely, traditional soaps there is a rehearsal day when the director and actors 'block' the script by working out where actors will stand when they deliver their lines, and work on interpretation of the script itself. This is when actors complain that they cannot say lines or do not understand them. The writer can attend blocking, and should do so. It is a salutary experience.

> Our audience is looking to see an immediacy and relevance to their lives, and this is particularly true among young people, for whom drama is one of their viewing preferences.
>
> (BBC Drama Department)
>
> I like to write with the world shut out and completely naked. Who knows – some of the stuff I write might not be as good if I had kept my kit on.
>
> (Al Hunter Ashton, *Eastenders* script writer)

15

Other Markets for Scripts

Almost all television work for freelance writers is in drama and situation comedy, but a few opportunities exist in other areas.

CHILDREN'S PROGRAMMES

Children's drama has been covered in Chapter 13. Otherwise opportunities are few. The BBC uses some unpublished stories and says that ideas for children's programmes will be considered. Writers, it is said, should watch the department's output carefully to see the types of programmes being made.

For ITV watch the output carefully, note which regional company (or Independent) is putting Children's ITV on the network, and then approach the executive producer directly.

EDUCATION

The BBC transmits more than 2,000 hours of educational programming each year, an amount roughly matched by ITV and Channel 4. Many schools programmes are drama or dramatised documentary and ought, in theory, to provide excellent opportunities for new writers. The BBC says, however, that most of its schools programmes are written either by the producer or by a teacher/academic who has been approached by the production team.

Apart from schools broadcasting, BBC Education is looking for history programmes that encourage an active interest by viewers, for programmes that deal with citizenship and the community, and for programmes that deal with parenting. Costs must be similar to daytime prices (see below).

For ITV and Channel 4 note the television companies making the programmes in which you are interested, and ring them directly (for contacts see Chapter 19).

SCIENCE PROGRAMMES

Most writers are expected to be involved with the actual production – which in practice means that writers are either BBC staff, or experts approached by either the production team or the independent production company that has been commissioned to make the programme. The BBC stresses, however, that consideration is given to scripts or ideas that are sent in. It is clearly an advantage to be an expert – if your idea is a programme showing the bizarre effects of quantum mechanics on daily life it is more likely to be taken seriously if you are a physicist rather than a stockbroker.

Treatments should be about two or three pages long, outlining the subject and making clear the way the writer would tackle the script.

HISTORY PROGRAMMES

The BBC and Channel 4 have discovered the appeal of history in recent years, and although most resources go into series like *Timeteam* and *Meet the Ancestors* there is a market for one-off features and part series, and these often include scripted sequences, even if it is only cavemen sitting round a fire going 'Ug'. If you have an idea for a history programme featuring dramatised sequences your best option is to approach an independent company that has a track record making historical documentaries. If they think the idea has appeal, they can put the proposal forward as a package.

LIGHT ENTERTAINMENT

Comedy sketch shows use a huge amount of material and there is a market for freelance sketches and one-liners. The BBC is at pains to say that 'there is no call for comic songs or verse'. Write directly to the producer of the show you are interested in, or to the head of light entertainment at ITV and Channel 4 and the BBC.

HUMAN INTEREST, CONSUMERS AND LEISURE

This is a vast and growing area of television. The enthusiasm for 'fly on the wall' documentaries that follow people about their daily lives has not passed, and there are innumerable cookery programmes, programmes about decorating and gardening, programmes about pets and vets, and specific interest programmes like *Sky at Night*,

Crimewatch UK, and *Holiday*. Sadly there is virtually no work here for the freelance writer, but new ideas are always wanted, and if they are taken up you can expect to be given every opportunity to script whatever needs scripting.

See which independent production companies are making the programmes you like, and approach them directly with your own idea.

DAYTIME TELEVISION

Daytime television is invariably low cost. In practice this means that the BBC expects to pay an independent company around £15,000 for a 30-minute programme. There is a market for documentary series (like *City Hospital*), panel games, quizzes, and interactive topical shows (i.e. chat shows). If you can come up with an idea for a 25–40 minute documentary type programme that only costs £4,000 then BBC 2 would love to hear from you (programmes in this area normally utilize news or sports archive material). Again, your best bet is to make an approach through an independent.

SCOTTISH, WELSH, IRISH AND REGIONAL PROGRAMMING

Both the BBC and ITV in Scotland, Wales and Ulster devote resources to programmes that will not be shown throughout the United Kingdom and which reflect Scottish, Welsh and Irish interests. The BBC, for example, makes about ten hours a week specifically for Scotland.

Watch output, identify the slots devoted to regional programming, and if you have an idea approach the producer.

All the main ITV companies make programmes for their own regions. The BBC makes specific regional programmes from Birmingham, Newcastle, Manchester, Bristol and Plymouth. Again, watch the regional slots (usually on BBC 2) and if you have an idea, write to the producer.

Telephone numbers for BBC and ITV production centres are included in Chapter 19.

> We aim to add more peak time talent to our schedule. We should also be a launch pad for bright, new talent both on-screen and off – a place of enterprise and creativity.
>
> (Jane Lush, Head of BBC Daytime Commissioning)

16

Common Queries

Should I include a list of characters at the front of the script?
Yes, but keep it short, don't worry about minor characters and make your descriptions pithy and pertinent. 'Julian is late forties, a chartered accountant, married for around 20 years to Rose. The only apparent interest in their lives is who will reach the menopause first.' Do not write half a page of description on each character, and do not insist that they be tall or short or red-haired or bald, unless this characteristic is vital to the story.

Should I include a synopsis of the story?
A short indication of what the play is about – perhaps 50 or 100 word – can be useful in that it tells the script editor the sort of play she is about to read. 'A man claiming to be an SAS agent breaks into a remote Welsh farmhouse. He tells the farmer and his family that he is being pursued by the IRA following a shooting in Northern Ireland. It sounds insane...but the telephone lines are cut and somebody is certainly watching the house...'

This gives the editor a good idea of what is to come – a drama about a family torn out of normality into a nightmare situation. She will go on reading to see how well or badly you tackle the subject.

Do not write a three- or four-page synopsis. The script editor or professional reader might just as well read the play, and anyway the reader will be required to write a synopsis to prove that she has read the script carefully.

Do I need to write 'copyright' and put a 'C' inside a circle?
It is curious but true that the very worst writers submitting the most unlikely scripts are those most anxious not to have their material stolen – and they very often put on their script a very firm copyright line. Very few professional writers or agents do this (your work is your copyright whether you draw little circles on it or not), although it is always a good idea to put the date on each draft you submit. If you want to protect your script further you can register it with the

Writer's Guild providing you are a member (see page 171), or you can seal a copy in an envelope and send it to yourself by registered mail, and then keep the package unopened.

Will my ideas be stolen?

If they are going to be stolen, a copyright line will not help you. Many unsuccessful writers are convinced that their ideas have been stolen and used later, and it is easy to see how suspicions are aroused. A writer sends in an outline for a series of dramas set in a university, say, and it is rejected. Then, a year later, a university series pops up on the *same channel* that rejected his idea!

There have always been university/student ideas floating around, just as there have always been outlines for series set in airports, hospitals, city parks, animal sanctuaries, riding stables, factories.... There have recently been two rival proposals for series set on trains.

It must have happened that a writer's work *has* been stolen but it is a very unlikely occurrence. Nobody is going to plagiarise an actual script – they have no need to. If your script is good they will buy it anyway, and besides you would be very likely to find out and complain. Again if your idea for a series is *very specific* nobody is going to be foolish enough to try to pass it off as their own.

There is, however, a grey area when it comes to ideas. Say you have submitted an idea for a comedy series about two rival pleasure boat operators on the Thames. The idea is read and rejected. A year later the editor who rejected you is involved in another project, and suddenly has a flash of brilliance: 'We could have a chap who hires rowing boats, and somebody could try to move in on his patch...'

The editor has probably no idea where the thought came from. Even if she does remember your offering she will not regard the idea as exclusively yours. Intellectual copyright is a very difficult area of law, but basically you cannot copyright ideas (unless they are worked out in detail) and you cannot copyright titles.

Are there rules about where to put the commercial break?

Officially, yes, but they are sometimes ignored. The established IBA rule is that the scene following a commercial break must be either (a) in a different location to the scene immediately before the commercial break, or (b) there must have been a time lapse of at least five minutes in your drama.

In other words you cannot do this:

DIANE: OK, right, so who is the little tart?

MARTIN: This is not doing any good, this is just upsetting you.

DIANE: Will you tell me who she is, damn you!

MARTIN LOOKS UP, SUDDENLY DEFIANT

MARTIN: OK, if you really want to know.

COMMERCIAL BREAK

SCENE FIVE. THE KITCHEN AS IN SCENE FOUR

MARTIN: The woman I am leaving you for is Lisa Strombali from the petfood factory.

DIANE: My best friend Lisa? You rat!

The scene before the commercial break is fine. After the break you would need to assume a short time lapse and preferably take us to a different location.

SCENE FIVE. EXT. PARK. DAY. DIANE IS LEANING OVER THE FOOTBRIDGE. MARTIN IS WITH HER.

DIANE: I suppose you met her at the petfood factory.

MARTIN: Yes.

And so on.

Must the commercial break be exactly halfway through the script?
It is more important that it should come at a natural, dramatically effective point.

That said, a 30-minute slot on ITV is just over 24 minutes long, and it is usual for the break to be somewhere in the middle four minutes.

A one-hour serial or series slot is 52 minutes long, and generally has two commercial breaks. The first should be at least 15 minutes into the script, and the last not less than 15 minutes from the end.

When submitting to the BBC *take the breaks out.*

How do I time my script?

If you follow either of the script layouts suggested in Figures 1 and 2 on pages 87 and 88 your script will be running at around 45 seconds a page – depending, of course, on the pace and mood of the play and the amount of description you include.

If you read your script out aloud (preferably with another person, alternating lines), and also *read out loud the movements of the characters and action sequences*, you will get a rough timing. Nobody expects more of you at this stage.

Why do television scripts only use the right-hand side of the page?

There are three versions of a television script.

1. The first is by the writer, and is written for the script editor and producer to read. There is no practical reason why this should only run down half the page – it is wasteful and leads to high postage costs. However, it is commonly done.

2. The second version is the rehearsal script, typed up by the production secretary after the first version has been edited, rewritten, changed for continuity, or cut for time. This version traditionally runs down the right-hand side of the page so that:

3. The director's PA can add the camera directions to the production secretary's word processor file without having to retype it. And in the studio or on location, the PA and floor managers can use the left-hand space to make continuity notes.

The examples in Figures 24, 25 and 26 are from a studio play, and show these three versions of the script.

What if my script is altered?

For a script editor to alter your script and rewrite bits presupposes that you are in the happy position of having sold it, that your script

3. CAFE
DAISY brings ANNA a coffee and sits with her.

DAISY
Did you go to the meeting? Did he ask you out?

ANNA
Yes I went and no he didn't. I don't know why - I can't understand it. I wore my best suit, you know, the pretend Chanel one with the little gold chains.

DAISY
To a CND meeting?

ANNA
There's no reason not to look my best, Daisy, whatever the occasion. And my black patent heels, because Simon's so tall I thought he wouldn't feel threatened.

DAISY

No. Well what happened?

ANNA
What happened? They kept talking about the bomb and all that sort of thing, that's what happened.

DAISY
They would at a CND meeting. I don't think you take it seriously.

ANNA chokes on her coffee.

ANNA
Seriously - my God I'm dead serious! I joined didn't I? If Simon doesn't ask me out soon I don't know what else I can do-

Fig. 24. A page as originally written.

SCENE 5 THE CAFE

DAISY
ANNA

DAISY
All I meant was he might notice you more if you could talk to him about his interests.

ANNA
I've joined CND. I went on a march - in my red slingbacks with four inch heels all through London, past all the shops and I didn't go in, not even down Sloane Street. I can talk about his interests. I don't suppose he's going to want me to know more about them than he does.

DAISY
No ---

ANNA
Men never do. He gave me a lift home after the meeting.

DAISY
You see! He must like you.

ANNA
He must, really, mustn't he. Well, I did ask him if he would. I left my car at home on purpose and said I had a tube phobia.

- 13 -

Fig. 25. The rehearsal script.

"FLOGGING A DEAD PRINCE"	SCENE 6
	DAISY COMES OVER WITH HER PAD.
	DAISY One egg mayonaise and salad, three coffees and a chocolate fudge cake.
See DAISY in + hold her away L to 2S DAISY/GIORGIO	GIORGIO We need more egg mayo, OK?
	DAISY GOES THROUGH TO THE KITCHEN.
52. 3 CU GIORGIO	GIORGIO I saw a traffic warden earlier. I hope your cab's all
53. 5 CU A?B	right out there. /
	BRIAN
54. 2 2S GIORGIO/MARIA	She won't bother my cab. What were we saying about Gustavus Adolphus. /
/5 repo KitchenL/	MARIA
Hold 2S with her cross	(PATIENTLY) Gustavus Adolphus, the Swedish Meteor, took Pomerania in 1630 only to face the obstacle of Brandenburg and Saxony.
	GIORGIO
Hold her away R to BRIAN & ease in to CU	(WHISPERS) Stop encouraging him.
	BRIAN That's right. Now then, a lot of people have got the wrong end of the stick about the 30 years war.
/SHOT 55 ON 5 NEXT/	END OF SCENE

Fig. 26. The camera script.

is in production and other creative influences are now at work.

Essentially, having accepted several thousand pounds for a script, it is no longer your property: at least not insofar as the rights you have sold are concerned. After all, if you buy a chair and take it home you can do what you like with it – chop a bit off one leg because of your uneven floor, or add a structural support – and you do not expect the carpenter to come and interfere and shout at you.

In practice, having bought the script the television company can cut it, but cannot *add lines* without informing you, the writer. You cannot actually stop them adding lines – but if you disagree strongly, you can take your name off the play.

How important are titles?

It is quite likely that the script editor will first open and start to read your script without even looking at the title. Many television plays – and in particular series – go through half a dozen titles (known as **working titles**) before the final name is agreed.

There is no doubt that a strong title is a good thing, and titles with sexual connotations and hints of intrigue always do well: *Blackeyes*, *Sleeping with the Enemy*, *The After Dinner Game*, *Too Hot to Handle*, *The Year of the Sex Olympics*. Action titles are good: *Licking Hitler* and *Spend, Spend, Spend* and titles that conjure up memorable images like *The Saliva Milkshake* and *Deadhead.* There is a theory in America that any title with a number in it cannot fail – *The Third Man*, *The Fourth Protocol*, *Beverley Hills 90210* – and indeed it is said that films are now being made with titles like *Godmother 6* without there having been any Godmothers one to five.

Do I need an agent?

A good agent is an enormous help. A good agent is known and respected by producers. When a script from such an agent arrives on a producer's desk it is taken seriously, read quickly, and the assumption right from the start is that it is good. Many programmes (like *The Bill*) say they will not look at a script at all unless it comes through an agent.

It is unlikely, as a new writer, that an agent can get you a higher fee than you could get for yourself. But an agent will make sure your residual rights and repeat fees are as they ought to be – particularly when dealing with independent production companies.

The problem is: how do you get a good agent to take you on? Good agents are careful to guard their reputation. They will not send a script to a producer unless they have confidence in it. They will not take on a writer unless they are confident in his ability. Persuading a decent agent to read your script and take you up is probably as difficult as getting a television company to buy your script in the first place.

If you approach a top television agent you are likely to be told that she already has more writers than she can handle, and is not looking for new clients at the moment. Occasionally this might be true. But at the end of the day all agents are interested in new, exciting writers – it is the ten per cent of your talent that keeps them fat and prosperous – and if you have genuine ability an agent will eventually take you up and devote much time and effort to helping you.

It is best to approach an agent once you have either:

- won a playwriting competition, particularly one for television, or a London pub theatre writing competition, *or*

- had at least one play – either for television or radio – accepted.

A list of agents dealing in TV scripts is on page 184.

How much will I be paid?

Writing for television is generally considered lucrative – but some slots pay a lot more than others, often because they attract automatic repeat fees. A good agent will fight to get you as much as possible, but most series and serials pay set rates, particularly for new writers. If you don't have an agent you can check on current agreements with the Writer's Guild or – a wise move – you can join the Society of Authors and they will check through your contract for you free of charge (see Chapter 18, page 170).

Some examples of television drama fees:

- A new writer will get around £5,000 for a 60-minute original television play on the BBC. This might sound a lot but is actually not much for many weeks of work.

- On the other hand, when repeat fees are taken into account, an established writer will get £5,000 for a single episode of *Coronation Street*.

- A 50-minute script in an ITV series like *London's Burning* will pay between £5,000 and £7,300 depending on how established you are.

- A 50-minute script for a BBC series like *Casualty* will pay between £4,000 and £6,000.
- Writers become 'established' after writing three or four scripts.
- The BBC generally pays at least £1,000 an hour less than ITV.
- Channel 5 pays less than either. An episode of *Family Affairs* will pay around half what a writer will get on *Emmerdale*.
- The ITV rate for children's drama and educational drama (both areas where new writers might find work) is £86.70 a minute. Religious drama, if there were ever to be any, would be paid at the same rate.
- When you are invited to attend the read-through of your script, and attend rehearsals, you will be paid £67 a day by the BBC and £75 a day by ITV (and in both cases you will be very unfortunate if the script editor doesn't take you to lunch).
- The most lucrative work is on serials like *Taggart* where one writer devises and scripts three one-hour episodes. This might pay up to £9,000 an episode, with the same again if the serial is repeated, and the possibility of as much again from overseas sales. Three scripts might thus earn £80,000 or more for a few weeks' work.
- A writer who spends three months of the year on a serial like *Coronation Street* and also writes for other programmes can comfortably earn £100,000 a year.
- If you are a poet, however, and one of your published poems is read on BBC television, you will be paid at the rate of £22.02 per half minute, and might well starve to death.

> From Daytime to late-peak we require innovation and invention, programmes that will stop a popular audience in their tracks or have them switch across to BBC 1 at key points every day.
>
> (Peter Salmon, Controller, BBC 1)

17

TV Talk: Common Words and Expressions Used in Scripts and in the Television Industry

Action props Props used by actors in the course of a scene – swords if there is a sword fight, pen and paper if the scene calls for them to be used. The food consumed on set is an action prop.

Ambient noise Background noise like traffic or air-conditioning. Often referred to as 'atmos'.

Backing In the studio a piece of scenery put behind a door so that we do not see the studio when characters go in and out. Windows on sets similarly have backing scenery.

BCU Big close up. The camera shows only part of the face or object.

Betacam SP Broadcast quality videotape, a format now commonly used for shooting drama.

Bible When a drama series is given the go-ahead the first thing to be commissioned from the creator is the Bible. This is a full format with story idea, setting, locations, notes on style, character notes and usually the initial storylines.

Binned A script is 'binned' if it is not acceptable and cannot be re-written. The writer will already have been paid 50 per cent of the fee, but will not be entitled to the 'second half fee' if the script is not accepted. In practice writers are often paid the full amount in order to shut them up.

Boom The microphone is held over the actors' heads

on a boom or poked towards them behind the furniture. If you see actors on location, strolling over the hills with not a boom in sight, it means that either the sound operator is disguised as a sheep or the actors are using radio microphones.

Camera script A studio script with the camera moves and technical directions on it. (See Figure 17, page 110.)

Captions Opening captions show the title of the play or series, the individual episode title if there is one, the creator, the leading actors and usually the writer.

Ciné-vérite Fly-on-the-wall documentary style, often involving a hand-held camera, giving a feeling of realism.

Credits The names of actors, production staff and crew, and usually the producer and director. It used to be the case that the director always had the final credit, on a caption all to himself, but television is increasingly a producers' medium, and producers (or executive producers) are commonly taking the last place. To achieve this without aggravation directors are now sometimes credited among the opening captions. They like this because it is what happens on feature films.

CU Close up. The face of a character or object fills the screen.

Cut away If you want to leave a scene or set for a moment, to indicate a time lapse perhaps, or remind us of things happening elsewhere, or to give pace to a scene, the quick shot of something else is called a cut away. For instance, a tense scene of a couple waiting for a blackmailer to turn up might be interspaced with cut aways to show the blackmailer in his car driving towards the house, parking, coming up to the door. Or a scene showing a character dashing to save a victim might include quick cut aways of the victim bound and gagged and suffering terrible things.

Day for night Filming on location at night is extremely expensive. Every shot has to be separately lit, which involves unbelievable numbers of electricians, exorbitant hire charges on lighting equipment, and massive overtime payments to the crew (this last item is changing as independent companies negotiate more effectively than the old ITV companies).

A traditional way to include night scenes on a low budget is to shoot during the day but with special filters on the camera. This day for night trick results in sequences that look murky and have strange colour tones. However skilled the cameraman, the sky is usually much too bright. Directors and producers dislike having to shoot day for night.

DBS Direct satellite broadcasting.

Digital editing It used to be that when you copied tape it lost quality – 'went down a generation' – but digital technology means that edits can be dissolved and then reformed as new. Practically all editing – sound and picture – is now done digitally. Editors can do marvellous things, but cynics note that editing tape now taken ten times as long and costs ten times as much as it did in the old days when you had a piece of film and a razor blade.

Dress A set is dressed when it has all its bits and pieces in place – cushions, tablecloth, ornaments, the movable items that have been stored away to stop them being stolen or damaged while the set was not being used.

Dry An actor dries when he totally forgets his lines.

Dubbing mixer Or sound supervisor. The person who mixes and adjusts sound effects, dialogue and music once the programme is filmed or recorded.

Ext or Int Exterior or interior.

Although still very commonly used, Int and Ext survive from the days when Int meant anything done in the studio, and Ext was the bit of exterior shooting to show characters out and about in the world.

Nowadays most dramas are shot entirely on location, either on film or video, and directions as to Int or Ext are often superfluous. The direction INT. JULIA'S BATHROOM is pointless, unless there is a possibility that Julia's bathroom might be open to the skies, or somebody might be clinging to the outside wall peering in. The description EXT. EXMOOR is eqully redundant, as INT. EXMOOR would be a nonsense. Int and Ext are still used, however.

Extras Actors who do not have lines and are not individually and specifically directed to carry out particular actions. People sitting drinking and chatting in the background of the Rover's Return are extras. Generally speaking writers need not worry about extras – the production will hire as many or few as it can afford. It is not a good idea, however, to write a play that positively must have a battalion of the Grenadier Guards milling around – you are likely to end up with four or five extras desperately trying to look like a battalion by moving about a lot.

Extras who are required to speak or to actually do something are called **walk ons**. A walk on can have ten words or so and can be directed. Thus if the barmaid in the Rover's Return says 'Now then Charlie, what was it a pint of mild?' and an extra nods and says, 'That's right' the extra will be classified as a walk on and be paid a few pounds more. Similarly if you want us to come across your hero entwined in the arms of a beautiful girl who is kissing him passionately and murmuring

'Cuddlebundle', the actress will be a walk on providing she does not say 'cuddlebundle' more than ten times and providing it is agreed that 'cuddlebundle' is one word and not two. The eleventh 'cuddlebundle' will officially, though not in practice, qualify her as a *speaking character* and put up her fee from around £70 to around £250. In practice actors are grateful for every word given because it increases their exposure on television.

Lines for a walk on should not be written in the script as dialogue but given to the actor on the day. You should thus write:

9. INT. DISCO. NIGHT

WE DISCOVER RORY IN CLOSE EMBRACE WITH YET ANOTHER BLONDE. SHE IS MURMURING WORDS OF ENDEARMENT AS MARIAN APPROACHES AND STARES AT THEM WITH A GRIM EXPRESSION.

Fade to black When you want the screen to go to black, often used between scenes as a time passage. This device used to be popular, then was regarded as terribly clumsy, and now is regarded by some as quite artistic. American dramas tend to fade to black every few minutes, but this is because the advertising breaks have been taken out.

Film editor The film editor or VT (videotape) editor assembles the programme from the material shot, usually under the instruction of the director. In film the first assembly or **rough cut** will be viewed by the producer and script editor, who make their comments. A writer should endeavour to be present at this stage, although there may be resistance.

Fluff When an actor muddles up a line or says the wrong word. An actor who does this will often do it again and again, at exactly the same place. Sometimes this is because of stress and tension –

studio time costs hundreds of pounds every minute – and sometimes because the line or word is genuinely difficult to say. 'Probably' is often a word to cause fluffs, and actors will always thank you for writing 'I expect I'll potter to Pettifers' rather than 'I'll probably potter to Pettifers'.

Footprint Satellites have different 'footprints' – their programmes can only be seen on television sets within their area of broadcasting as they travel round the Earth.

Format A document explaining an idea for a series or soap opera. A format is usually about ten pages long. A shorter document of two or three pages might be called an **outline**. Nobody knows which term is correct and nobody really cares. (See also **Bible**.)

Genre A type of programme. Soap opera is a genre. So is science fiction. Critics, script editors, director and producers are all fond of the word.

Gun mike A microphone that operates in a very narrow band, but over a long distance. It can be used to pick up the speech of an individual in a crowd.

High angle shot/ low angle shot The camera looking down or looking up.

Indie Independent production companies are known as Indies. Twenty-five per cent of television production is supposed to be made by Indies. Some of them are very big like Working Title and Pearson, but others are very small – often just one or two hopeful people working from home with a phone, fax, and headed notepaper saying Megaworld Productions UK Ltd.

In frame A person or object is in the camera's view.

In the can A scene that is 'in the can' has been successfully (technically, if not artistically) recorded or filmed.

Libel

When your script is commissioned you will sign a contract stating that you will use your best endeavours to ensure that no defamatory matter is included in your work. The most obvious danger of libel comes from the choice of a character's name, or the name of a place. On page 25 there is an outline for a play about a man called Slime who starves to death the residents of the Hardtimes Residential Home for the Elderly. If this play were transmitted and it transpired that there really was a Mr Slime in charge of a Hardtimes Residential Home for the Elderly then he would be likely to claim damages for defamation of character.

The trouble with a real television play is that you cannot fall back on patently invented names like Slime.

So what can you do to protect yourself? Basically, you should be certain that you have *not* libelled somebody you know. If there is an accountant called Fidgetwig living next to you, do not write a play about a crooked wife-beating animal-loathing accountant called Fodgetwog, because your neighbour will successfully sue you and the television company for a large amount of money.

In practice the script editor will carry out what is called a **neg check**. Thus if you have a crooked security organisation in your play a check will be made (there are specialist firms who do this) on company registers to make sure that no security organisation with the name you have chosen actually exists.

Using a very common name is not necessarily a protection. It is true that if you call a sex maniac teacher Smith, you will not be liable for prosecution by the thousands of teachers called Smith in Britain. But if your play is about a sex maniac teacher Smith who has four daughters, a water spaniel and a Volvo and lives in Chipping Dodsbury, and after transmission you get a call from a Mr Smith of Chipping Dodsbury who has four daughters, a King Charles Spaniel and a Saab – then you are in big trouble.

Again, though, the television company will in practice have done a neg check on teachers in the Chipping Dodsbury locality.

Library film Film or videotape material not shot specifically for your play. If you have a scene with a teacher explaining the life cycle of the kangaroo, you might ask to see library film of kangaroos on a video screen behind the teacher's head. Use of library film is costed at so much per second, and the price depends on whether the production needs UK rights or world rights. Don't write it in without consulting the script editor.

LS Long shot – figures in distance, obviously not possible in a studio production.

Mix **Cross fade** as it is known in radio, or **dissolve** on film, is when one scene merges gently into the next rather than a straight **cut**.

MLS Medium long shot – generally a group of figures.

MS Mid shot – this would show figures from about the waist up.

Narrative The narrative is the story told through the plot. It is what happens scene by scene, and when script editors says a script has a strong narrative they mean that on the superficial storytelling level it holds their attention and develops well.

A script can have a strong narrative and still be empty of new ideas or originality.

OB Filmed, or recorded on video, away from the studio.

Off the page Good dialogue is said to come 'off the page' – it has energy and life and is believable. It is very bad news when a script editor says: 'This dialogue just doesn't come off the page'.

Option If a television company or independent production company wants to adapt a novel they first take out an option with the copyright owner, usually the writer. Even small independent production companies take out options, as this then gives them a 'property' that nobody else can touch during the period of the option. (See page 119.)

Offline edit Working on videotape rather than film, the director uses a small offline edit suite to produce the equivalent of a film rough cut or first assembly. This saves time when the director moves into the vastly more expensive **online edit suite** where the final editing actually takes place.

OOV Out of vision. Sometimes called **OS** (**off screen**). We are listening to a character who is in the scene but is not visible. (But see VO below.)

Pan The camera remains in a static position but the lens moves along a row of people, round a room, or across a landscape. The camera does not change its focus.

POV The camera shows us something from a particular character's point of view.

Producer's run When studio plays (nowadays mainly soap operas) have been rehearsed and actors are 'off the book' (know their lines) the play is run through without costumes or cameras for the producer and script editor to watch. At this point the producer can cut things and change interpretations she does not like, and the script editor can insist that the actors go back to the lines that were written for them, rather than the ones they've made up in rehearsal.

Production values Are what everybody wants. If a show has good production values it means that visually the budget is being well spent, that the show looks lavish and interesting without costing an arm and a leg.

Pull back The camera pulls back from a close up or medium shot to show more of the scene.

Reader Most ITV companies and large independent production companies employ readers to assess unsolicited scripts. These readers are often would-be script editors, usually female, often not long out of university. They are paid anything between £20 and £75 to read your script. They then have to summarise the story (to prove they have read it through) and give their opinion in around 100 words. Readers are sometimes more skilled and perceptive than you might expect.

Read through On the first day of production the cast, technical staff, production staff and the writer come together for the first time, to read through the play. Whilst some actors are happy to give a performance, others read through the lines in a dull monotone. This is not because they dislike the play, but because they dislike interpreting the lines before rehearsal.

Residuals The extra money you get when your play is repeated in the UK or sold elsewhere in the world. (See **How much will I be paid?**, page 151.)

Script unit The BBC has a comedy script unit and the bigger ITV companies and Indies have heads of drama development (often young graduates from Oxford who want to work in television). Readers are employed to process unsolicited material (see Chapter 19). Often they will give useful advice if they think you show ability. Unlike script editors assigned to particular programmes, who are paid to find an exact number of scripts to fill an exact number of slots and do not have time or inclination to run a free advice service, script editors working with script units have a duty to encourage and help promising talent.

The drawback is that however much a script unit editor likes your work she is never in a position actually to *buy it*. At the end of the day it is a producer or editor working on a series that you have to please.

SFX Sound effects. Denotes a particular sound effect that you want over a shot – if somebody is lying in bed dreaming about the sea and you want the sound of seagulls it would be an SFX. Rather old-fashioned radio phrase – it is as easy to write 'We hear the sound of seagulls and crashing waves'.

Slow zoom The camera moves slowly in.

Stock shot A shot that can be used over and over again. Often a three- or four-second shot of the exterior of a house in a series or serial drama.

Storyline In series drama, a storyline is what the writer submits. It gives the basic story and shows the development of the plot stage by stage. In soap operas the storyline is drawn up by the script editors and details the stories that will be covered by individual writers. (See page 99).

Talking heads A play in which people talk to each other all the time, in boring locations, without any action. 'Talking heads' is generally regarded as a pejorative expression. 'It's nothing but talking heads' a director will moan.

Tighten A zoom in, but gently and not as dramatic or as much.

Tracking shot The camera moves with the characters – perhaps two people walking towards us, and the camera moving away at the same speed. The camera itself can also track in on a group. This is different from the **zoom** in that the camera itself moves, so that the angle on the subjects changes. We might, for example, start on the backs of the two characters as they sit on a sofa, and then track round with the camera until we see their faces.

Treatment Development of an idea, showing how it will break down scene by scene, and often including examples of dialogue.

Two hander A scene with only two characters.

Two shot (2S) Two people on the screen.

VO Voice over. A narrator voicing over a scene in a sound studio, or dialogue from scene A that is put over scene B for artistic effect.

Whip pan A pan at speed – again not used in studio and only when being artistic on film.

Working title If a writer cannot think up a good title for a play or series he gives it a working title just to be going on with. On the first page this will be indicated by:

BOOT MAN
(Working Title)
by Veronica Jane Rumble

Wrap The time recording or filming ends. A location will wrap at a certain time. 'It's a wrap' means that shooting has finished for the day. 'We wrapped at one minute to six,' says the production manager to the associate producer, who is worried about overtime.

Zoom The camera focus moves in or out on a person or object.

18

Organisations that will Help You

- Writing courses and workshops.
- Internet-based courses and workshops.
- Internet help sites for new writers.
- Writers' organisations.
- University courses.
- Arts associations.

WRITING COURSES AND WORKSHOPS

Your aim, at all times, should be to *make contact with a professional, working, script editor*. Sending a script cold through the post might be your only option if you live in remote Wales or the Orkneys (where script editors rarely stray in a professional capacity) but for those able to do so, attending scriptwriting courses can prove fruitful. Here are some recent examples:

- A biochemist with no contacts in the television world attended a weekend writing seminar in the Cotswolds (advertised in the *Guardian*) and her script was assessed by a professional working script editor. She went on to write for *Eastenders*.
- Three young graduates on a scriptwriting course at the Northern Media School, Sheffield, were among students who had their work assessed by an assistant producer from Channel 5. They were all offered contracts on *Family Affairs*.
- A young playwright attended a TV-writing course organised at the Liverpool Playhouse. His script was read by a senior script editor from Thames TV. He is now writing for *The Bill*.

When you consider a scriptwriting course of any kind you should always look carefully at the quality of advice you will be getting.

- DO go for scriptwriting courses where your work will be looked at by professionals currently working in the industry. Always, if you can, opt for a course where you meet your tutor.
- BE WARY OF courses where the tutors are media-course academics who have never actually worked in television – or are said to have had a distinguished career as script consultants on TV drama in the 1960s.
- BE VERY WARY OF correspondence courses. Quality of advice can be very uneven. You might be given an able tutor who has recently worked in television, but you might equally get somebody who has hardly worked in the business at all. Always ask to be told your tutor's credits. Avoid courses which ask you to do 'exercises' or to keep revising a piece of work. Some of the correspondence writing schools that advertise 'your money back if you have not sold a script by the end of the course' are reputable and give sound advice – but clearly, there are not many people who ever finish their courses. You are better off improving your skills by writing new ten-minute dramas that have a chance of being bought and made into programmes.
- Quality advice is not always cheap. A professional script editor or producer working on a major top-20 series is not going to assess scripts by unknown authors for £5 an hour. Consultancies can charge up to £100 for a full script analysis. Some residential weekends cost over £300. On the other hand, professional working script editors sometimes attend seminars and short courses run by arts associations or universities. These might be free to local aspiring writers.
- Check your local arts association on forthcoming scriptwriting courses (often run by university departments of continuing education) and with writers' organisations in your area.
- Look out for scriptwriting courses advertised in the press (usually the *Guardian* media pages).

Residential courses and workshops

Residential writing courses and workshops are often run by enthusiasts and can be excellent – but often they survive for only a few years and then, sadly, fade away. As with everything else, check on the Internet to see what is on offer. Two organisations that have a long track record and high reputation are the Arvon Foundation and the Screenwriters' Workshop.

The Arvon Foundation

High quality tutors run five-day residential courses at Hebden Bridge in Yorkshire, Totleigh Barton in Devon, and Beauly in Inverness-shire. The foundation runs courses in many forms of creative writing, including film scriptwriting and television drama. Courses are informal and friendly – students and tutors make their own breakfasts and lunches and share the cooking of the evening meal – and are open to anybody over the age of 16. The foundation is supported by the English and Scottish Arts Councils and the fees are low – around £350 including accommodation and food.

The Arvon Foundation
Totleigh Barton
Sheepwash
Devon EX21 5NS
Tel: (01409) 231338
Website: *www.arvonfoundation.org/index*

The Screenwriters' Workshop

Formerly the London Screenwriters' Workshop, it helps new writers with seminars, workshop events and tuition. The largest organisation of its kind in Europe, the Workshop now receives funding from the European Union (EU). It was founded in 1983 by a group of film and television writers as a forum for contact, discussion, and practical criticism. Courses cover every aspect of scriptwriting, from how to write a treatment to how to do a rewrite. Some courses last for several weeks, other subjects are covered in afternoon or evening workshops. There is also a script-reading service that offers a professional assessment of your script with suggestions on story-lines, character, plot and dialogue.

Membership Secretary
Screenwriters' Workshop
114 Whitfield Street
London
W1P 5RW
Tel: (020) 7387 5511
Website: *www.lsw.org.uk*

Euroscript

An EU scheme to promote European scriptwriting. It provides funding to develop five screenplays a year, and if you are a successful applicant you will be given your own script editor and, if necessary, cash for travel and subsistence. The organisation also runs workshops and provides support for writers' groups, and offers 'a full in-depth written script analysis' service for £95 a script. In the UK it lives at the same address as the Screenwriters' Workshop (see above).

Tel: (020) 7387 5880
Website: *www.euroscript.co.uk*

Comedy

Carlton comedy writing course
Carlton Television has run a comedy writing course for several years, designed to provide a solid grounding for writers new to television and 'give them a comprehensive understanding of the development process'. Only new writers are taken on the course, the intention is to have a marketable script at the end of it, and there's even a fee of £1000. Write for details to:

Comedy Department
Carlton Television
33–38 Portman Square
London W1H 9FM
Tel: (020) 7486 6688

Science-based drama

The PAWS Drama Fund
Although not strictly a workshop, the PAWS (Public Awareness of Science) drama fund gives grants to writers who come up with good ideas for science-based television drama, and also organises informal discussion evenings where scientists outline areas of their work they believe have dramatic potential, and television drama producers add their comments. There is generally an opportunity for writers to talk informally to both the scientists and the television people (it's the television people you want to meet!). PAWS is supported by companies like Zeneca, BP and Unilever. For details write to:

The PAWS Office
Osborne House
111 Bartholomew Rd
London NW5 2BJ

INTERNET-BASED COURSES AND WORKSHOPS

- **Situations Vacant** (*www.sitsvac.org*) gives information about workshops, sitcom pilots and scripts.
- **BBC Comedy Zone** (*www.comedyzone.beeb.com*) says that its online scriptwriting workshop will provide an introduction to the relevant steps involved in completing a half-hour sitcom, and give less experienced writers an organised and disciplined approach to their craft.
- **TV Scriptwriter** (*www.scriptwriter.org*) provides free advice on characterisation, construction, dialogue, etc. (adapted from this book) and offers a writing course tutored by script editors who have worked on mainstream TV programmes. Professional script assessments are sometimes on offer.
- **Virtual Script Workshop** (*www.xerif.com*) has links to various workshops for screenwriters, including sites in Hong Kong and Singapore.
- **Birkbeck College** at the University of London (*www.bbk.ac.uk*) offers two screenwriting courses on the Internet, one for beginners and one for more advanced students. Each course lasts ten weeks.
- **Gotham Writers' Workshop** (*www.write.org*) is perhaps the best American site offering online classes and tuition. You can access a free example of a television scriptwriting lecture.
- **The Jarvis Method** (*www.writerspage.com*) is another American site offering online seminars, although you have to be a night-owl as they don't finish until 5pm Pacific Time, which means 1am GMT.
- **TV Writer University** (*www.tvwriter.com*) also offers online seminars (this time at 3am GMT) and also offers script assessments by an American story editor for those who want to try the US market.

INTERNET HELP SITES FOR NEW WRITERS

- **Writing for Performance** (*www.kelly.mcmail.com*) gives valuable free advice and links to other sites.
- **Writernet** (*www.writernet.co.uk*) is designed to provide a

comprehensive service both for writers and producers and covers theatre, television and film.

- **Farnham Films** (*www.farnfilm.com*) is one of the most useful sites on the net. It provides a list of TV drama commissioning editors – invaluable as the list is regularly updated – and has plenty of advice for new writers. It also has a 'story machine' script that you can add to yourself.
- **The Screenwriters' Workshop** (*www.lsw.org.uk*) provides links to many local scriptwriter groups that can provide help with dialogue, style, structure, and characterisation through the positive criticism of fellow writers.
- **BBC Education** (*www.bbc.co.uk/education*) provides details of scriptwriting courses at various locations in the UK and Ireland.
- **Inkspot** (*www.inkspot.com*) is an American writers' resource site.

WRITERS' ORGANISATIONS

The Society of Authors

The society has an active broadcasting section with more than 800 members. There are occasional talks given by people working in the television industry – often producers and editors. It has a permanent staff, including a solicitor who will vet contracts for you (useful if you do not have an agent). The society will take legal action on your behalf if the issue is considered of general concern to the profession. The society's magazine *The Author* comes out four times a year and has a broadcasting section which sometimes gives information about scripts in demand. The society also publishes free guides on such subjects as television agreements, copyright, libel and authors' agents. If you do not qualify for membership of the society (you need to have had work accepted for publication or broadcast) you can buy *The Author* on subscription. There is also a category of associate membership for those who have not yet had a full-length work broadcast but have either received a major contract or have had occasional items broadcast. More information can be obtained from:

The Society of Authors
84 Drayton Gardens
London SW10 9SB
Tel: (020) 7376 6642
Website: *www.writers.org.uk/society*

The Writers' Guild of Great Britain
This is the writers' trade union and is affiliated to the TUC. It negotiates television fees (and radio fees jointly with the Society of Authors) and gives help and advice on everything from contracts and agents to fees. The Guild holds frequent meetings for members, and publishes a very useful range of booklets. If you are not a professional writer, the Guild has a category of membership specifically for those 'who are taking their first steps in writing but who have not as yet received a contract'. For information on membership, contact:

Writers' Guild
430 Edgware Road
London W2 1EH
Tel: (020) 7723 8074
Website: *www.writers.org.uk/guild*

UNIVERSITY COURSES

A number of universities offer courses in scriptwriting. Here are some of the better established.

- **Birmingham University** runs courses on writing play scripts for beginners at locations throughout the West Midlands.

  School of Continuing Studies
  Edgbaston
  Birmingham B15 2TT
  Tel: (0121) 414 5607

- **University of East Anglia**, famous for its MA programme in fiction, also runs courses in script and screenwriting.

  School of English and American Studies
  Norwich
  Norfolk NR4 7TJ
  Tel: (01603) 593262

- **Edinburgh University** offers summer schools in playwriting at which beginners are welcome.

  Centre for Continuing Education
  11 Buccleuch Place
  Edinburgh EH8 9LW
  Tel: (0131) 640 4400

- **Lancaster University** offers graduate and undergraduate courses.

  Department of Creative Writing
  Lonsdale College
  Bailrigg
  Lancaster LA1 4YN
  Tel: (01524) 596169

- **Northern School of Film and Television** offers a Postgraduate Diploma MA course in screenwriting. Recent graduates have gone on to write for programmes like *The Bill*, *Emmerdale* and *Coronation Street*.

  2 Queen Square
  Leeds
  West Yorkshire LS2 8AF
  Tel: (0113) 2831900
  Website: *www.lmu.ac.uk*

- **Nottingham Trent University** offers undergraduate and graduate courses in writing and scriptwriting.

  Humanities Faculty Office
  Clifton Lane
  Nottingham NG11 8NS
  Tel: (0115) 941 8418

- **Sheffield Hallam University** which also runs the **Northern Media School** offers courses in creative writing, scriptwriting and film studies.

  School of Cultural Studies
  Sheffield Hallam University
  Psalter Lane
  Sheffield S11 8UZ
  Tel: (0114) 225 5555

ARTS ASSOCIATIONS

Funded by the Arts Council and local authorities, often managing to dip their fingers into the European Union moneypot, these bodies have no other aim in life than to encourage the arts – in other words, as far as you are concerned, to provide new writers with subsidised seminars, writing courses, commissions and bursaries. Different arts associations vary in the amount of money and resources they allocate to new writers – some have been known to co-fund television productions with the BBC and Channel 4, others are less bold in their commitment. They all ought to keep an up-to-date list of organisations helpful to writers in their area.

England

East Midlands Arts
Leicestershire, Nottinghamshire, Derbyshire (but not the Peak District) and Northamptonshire. Address: Mountfields House, Epinal Way, Loughborough, Leicestershire LE11 0QE. Tel: (01509) 218292.

Eastern Arts
Bedfordshire, Cambridgeshire, Essex, Hertfordshire, Norfolk, Suffolk and Lincolnshire. Address: Cherry Hinton Hall, Cambridge CB1 4DW. Tel: (01223) 248075.

London Arts
Elm House, 3rd Floor, 133 Long Acre, London WC2E 9AF. Tel: (020) 7240 1313.

North West Arts
Lancashire, Cheshire, Greater Manchester, Merseyside and High Peak district of Derbyshire. Address: Manchester House, 22 Bridge Street, Manchester M3 3AB. Tel: (0161) 834 6644.

Northern Arts
Cumbria, Durham, Northumberland, Teesside, Tyne and Wear. Address: 9–10 Osborne Terrace, Jesmond, Newcastle upon Tyne NE2 1NZ. Tel: (0191) 281 6334.

South East Arts
Sussex, Kent, Surrey – but not the London boroughs. Address: 10 Mount Ephraim, Tunbridge Wells, Kent TN4 8AS. Tel: (01892) 515210.

South West Arts
Gloucestershire, Somerset, Devon, Cornwall, Dorset excluding Bournemouth and Poole. Address: Bradninch Place, Gandy Street, Exeter, Devon EX4 3LS. Tel: (01392) 218188.

Southern Arts
Berkshire, Buckinghamshire, Oxfordshire, Hampshire, Wiltshire, South East Dorset, the Isle of Wight. Address: 13 St Clement Street, Winchester, Hampshire SO23 9DQ. Tel: (01962) 855099.

West Midland Arts
West Midlands, Shropshire, Hereford and Worcester, Warwickshire, Staffordshire. Address: 82 Granville Street, Birmingham B1 2LH. Tel: (0121) 631 3121.

Yorkshire Arts
21 Bond Street, Dewsbury, West Yorkshire WF13 1AY. Tel: (01924) 455555.

Northern Ireland

Arts Council of Northern Ireland
185 Stranmillis Road, Belfast BT9 5DU. Tel: (028) 9038 1591.

Scotland

Scottish Arts
12 Manor Place, Edinburgh EH3 7DD.

Wales

Arts Council of Wales
Museum Place, Cardiff CF1 3NX. Tel: (029) 2039 4711.
North Wales Office: 10 Wellfield House, Bangor, Gwynedd LL57 1ER. Tel: (01248) 353248. *South East Wales Office*: Victoria Street, Cwmbran, Gwent NP44 3YT. Tel: (01633) 875075. *West Wales Office*: 6 Gardd Llydaw, Jacksons Lane, Carmarthen SA31 1QD. Tel: (01267) 234248.

> Writing is more than anything a compulsion, like some people wash their hands thirty times a day for fear of awful consequences if they do not. It pays a whole lot better than this type of compulsion, but it is no more heroic.
>
> (Julie Burchill)

19

Where to Send your Script

APPROACHING A SPECIFIC SCRIPT EDITOR

- Decide on the programme you want to write for. Also check Internet sites (see Chapter 18) that carry information on programmes looking for writers.
- Try to find out the name of the script editor or script executive – either by a telephone call to the programme company switchboard or by looking at the company's website.
- If you are a bold person, phone the programme company and in a confident voice ask to speak to the script editor by name. Nine times out of ten you will not be put through, but you might be lucky. If you are, tell them you know they've got plenty of writers, but you would be grateful for any advice – do they perhaps have a writers' pack that they could send you? Try to engage their sympathy without irritating them. Ask if they will look at a script as an example of your work.
- Whether you have made contact or not, send your script directly to the person you want to read it. If you've spoken to them on the phone, make your letter personal. ('Thank you for your advice. As discussed on the phone, here's my script *Happy Days*. It was good of you to offer to read it.') Keep your letter short but friendly.
- A good excuse for a phone call is to check on any special seasons for new writing or directing talent, or to ask if the company produces a writers' pack for a particular programme.

The Don't list

- Don't send a tatty manuscript decorated with coffee ring stains.
- Don't tell the script reader things about yourself that are not relevant, e.g. the funny incident at Ibiza that first made you become interested in writing; the friends who said 'You've got a

real gift for words.'

- Don't mention that your script has been turned down by others, e.g. 'Morag Veryweary at Central TV read *Happy Days* with interest but unfortunately was not producing plays of this type at the moment and regretfully had to return it to me. Nat Goaway at Granada also liked it very much but felt he had to return it as he would not have a slot until Autumn 2049....'

Main drama department addresses are listed below, as are the names of drama department contacts. Before sending in your script telephone to make sure that the office holders have not changed (a good website for this is *www.farnfilm.com*).

BBC CONTACT ADDRESSES

Drama

BBC Television Centre, Wood Lane, London W12 7RJ. Tel: (020) 8743 8000
Head of Single Drama and Films: David Thompson
Head of Serials: Jane Tranter
Executive Producer: BBC 2 serials: Hilary Salmon
Head of Series: Mal Young
Head of Development (series): Serena Cullen
NOTE: Serina Cullen is charged with 'spearheading a drive to find and invest in new talent'.

Childrens' drama

BBC Television Centre, Wood Lane, London W12 7RJ. Tel: (020) 8743 8000
Head of Children's Programmes: Lorraine Heggessey
Executive Producer, Drama: Elaine Sperber
Producer, *Grange Hill*: Jo Ward

Comedy

BBC Television Centre, Wood Lane, London W12 7RJ. Tel: (020) 8743 8000
Controller, BBC Entertainment: Paul Jackson
Head of Comedy: Geoffrey Perkins
Script Executive: Bill Dare
Send your script to the Comedy Script Unit: BBC Television Centre, Room 4006, Wood lane, London W12 7RJ. Website: *www.comedyzone.beeb.com*

Education

BBC White City, 201 Wood Lane, London W12 7TS. Tel: (020) 8752 5252
Director of Education: Marilyn Wheatcroft
Executive Producers: Clare Elstow, Geoff Marshall-Taylor, Sue Nott

BBC Birmingham

Broadcasting Centre, Pebble Mill Road, Birmingham B5 7QQ. Tel: (0121) 414 8888
Television Drama: Geoff Pope
Drama Series: Richard Langridge

Northern Ireland

Broadcasting House, Belfast BT2 8HQ. Tel: (028) 9033 8000
Head of Broadcast: Anna Carragher
Head of Drama: Robert Cooper

Scotland

Broadcasting House, Queen Margaret Drive, Glasgow G12 8DG. Tel: (0141) 339 8844
Head of Drama: Barbara McKissack
Head of Children's Programmes and Features: Liz Scott

Wales

Broadcasting House, Llandaff, Cardiff CF5 2YQ. Tel: (029) 2032 2000
Head of Broadcast (English language): Dai Smith
Head of Broadcast (Welsh language): Gwynn Pritchard
Head of Drama: Matthew Robinson

ITV CONTACT ADDRESSES

Anglia Television Ltd

Anglia House, Norwich NR1 3JG. Tel: (01603) 615 151. Website: *www.anglia.tv.co.uk*. Anglia produces some drama for the network (*Where the Heart Is* and *Touching Evil*) and will consider ideas. Do not send scripts until your idea has been discussed.

Carlton Productions

35–38 Portman Square, London W1H 9FH. Tel: (020) 7486 6688
Website: *www.carltontv.co.uk*
Head of Drama: Jonathan Powell

Executive Producers, Drama: Rob Pursey, Sharon Bloom
Controller of Comedy: Nick Symons
Children's Programmes: Michael Forte
Development Executive, Carlton Films: Tracey Jack
Makes a lot of mainstream drama for ITV including *Peak Practice*. Tries to use new writers on established long-running series. Its comedy department runs the Carlton sitcom course.

Central Broadcasting
Central House, Broad Street, Birmingham B1 2JP. Tel: (0121) 643 9898. Website: *www.carltontv.co.uk*
Central is now part of Carlton Television.

Granada Television Ltd
Granada Television Centre, Manchester M60 9EA. Tel: (0161) 832 7211
36 Golden Square, London W1R 4AH. Tel: (020) 7734 8080
Website: *www.granadatv.co.uk*
Head of International Drama: Antony Root
Head of Granada Films: Pippa Cross
Drama: Simon Lewis and Sally Hogg
Executive Producer, Comedy: Andy Harries
Children's and Youth Programmes: Stephen Andrew
Makes a huge amount of drama, including *Coronation Street*, for ITV, Channel 4 and the BBC.

Grampian Television
Queen's Cross, Aberdeen AB15 4XJ. Tel: (01224) 846 846. Website: *www.scottishmediagroup.com*
Controller: Derrick Thomson
Might be interested in fostering and supporting local writing talent.

HTV Ltd
HTV Wales, The Television Centre, Culverhouse Cross, Cardiff CF5 6XJ. Tel: (029) 2059 0590
HTV West, The Television Centre, Bristol BS4 3HG. Tel: (0117) 972 2722. Website: *www.htv.co.uk*
Controller of Children's Programmes: Dan Maddicott
Drama (Wales): Peter Edwards
Director of Programmes, Partridge Films: Michael Roseberg
Head of Development, Indie Productions: Sue Shephard
Now part of United News and Media. Makes drama and children's

programmes for the UK and the international market.

LWT

The London Television Centre, Upper Ground, London SE1 9LT. Tel: (020) 7620 1620. Website: *www.lwt.co.uk*
Controller of Entertainment: Nigel Lythgoe
Drama: Laura Mackie
Comedy: Lisa Clark, Humphrey Barclay
Development Consultant: Sarah Williams
Makes a lot of ITV drama programmes, including *London's Burning*. Will read unsolicited scripts, and give feedback and help to new writers that 'show exceptional talent'. Looking for sitcoms, 30-minute filmed comedy drama series, and one-off comedy films.

Meridian Broadcasting

Television Centre, Southampton, Hampshire SO14 0PZ. Tel: (023) 8022 2555. Website: *www.meridian.tv.co.uk*
Director of Programmes: Richard Simons
Has made drama in the past.

Scottish Television

Cowcaddens, Glasgow G2 3PR. Tel: (0141) 300 3000. Website: *www.stv.co.uk*
Controller of Drama: Philip Hinchcliffe
Makes drama and children's programmes for the ITV network, including *Taggart and McCallum*. Ideas for long-running series and serials are said to be welcome.

Tyne Tees Television Ltd

The Television Centre, City Road, Newcastle upon Tyne NE1 2AL. Tel: (0191) 261 0181. Website: *www.granadamedia.com*
Controller of Drama, Yorkshire Tyne Tees Productions: Keith Richardson
Now part of the Granada group.

Yorkshire Television Ltd

The Television Centre, Leeds LS3 1JS. Tel: (0113) 243 8283. Website: *www.granadamedia.com*
Controller of Comedy: Paul Spencer
Executive Producer, Entertainment: Jim Brown
Controller of Drama: Carolyn Reynolds
Controller of Comedy Drama: David Reynolds

CHANNEL 4 TELEVISION

124 Horseferry Road, London SW1P 2TX. Tel: (020) 7396 4444. Website: *www.channel4.com*
Head of Drama: Gub Neal
Commissioning Editor, Series: Catriona McKenzie
Commissioning Editor, Serials: Jonathan Young
Deputy Commissioning Editor: Jessica Pope
Channel 4 commissions programmes from independent companies and buys in ready-made programmes, but does not make programmes itself. It does, however, foster ideas and new writing talent. FilmFour Lab has a talent scout (Nic Murison) who actively seeks interesting ('cutting edge') new writers, directors and producers. Channel 4's remit is to provide programmes of interest to minority audiences and to be distinct and different from other channels.

Channel 4 says it is looking for 'ideas for series of four or six hour-long episodes written by single authors, which communicate an individual voice and have a real sense of vision'. It is also looking for three- or four-part mini-series that put a 'contemporary spin on genres such as romance or thrillers'.

In other words, it wants mass-audience stories of passion and intrigue that say something about life today.

For an update of the current situation phone and ask for a copy of Channel 4's *Writing Proposals for Channel 4: A guide for beginners*.

CHANNEL 5

22 Long Acre, London WC2E 9LY. Tel: (020) 7497 5225. Website: *www.channel5.co.uk*
Controller of Drama: Corinne Hollingworth
As with Channel 4, Channel 5 does not make programmes but commissions from independent programme makers. It has more than doubled its drama output and is interested in developing single drama and series.

BSKYB

Grant Way, Isleworth, Middlesex TW7 5QD. Tel: (020) 7705 3000. Now making a profit, there are hopes that BskyB will plough money back into drama commissioned from independents.

INDEPENDENT PRODUCTION COMPANIES

Some independents – for instance Pearson Television which makes drama series like *The Bill* and comedies like *Goodnight Sweetheart* – are bigger and more important than many of the individual ITV companies. Other independents are one-person affairs that occupy West End offices when they're in production, and shrink back into the spare bedroom in Hendon when they're back 'in development'. Big or small, however, there is little enthusiasm for reading unsolicited scripts and offering constructive advice to new writers.

WARNING: Beware of independent production companies that want you to develop your work without a fee. A company might well say: 'Get this script right and we'll bust a gut trying to get it on. . . .' Busting a gut in this context means that you spend weeks revising your script and the independent producer takes a Channel 4 commissioning editor to lunch and rapidly pitches a dozen different projects – including yours – in the hope that *one* goes forward into development. Too many writers are hacking away for nothing, paid only with words of encouragement and visions of hope. A company that really believes in your script will put money on the table.

Here are some of the more important of the 'indies'.

Channel X Communications

22 Stephenson Way, London NW1 2HD. Tel: (020) 787 3874.
E-mail: *mail@channelx.co.uk*
Contact: Alan Mark
Has made *Jo Brand – through the Cakehole* and *One for the Road* and is looking for situation comedies and comedy drama. Says it will look at a treatment and part-script in the first instance, and will help develop writers who show potential.

Hartswood Films

Twickenham Studios, The Barons, St Margaret's, Middlesex TW1 2AW. Tel: (020) 8607 8736
Contact: Elaine Cameron
Made *Men Behaving Badly* and *A Woman's Guide to Adultery.*

Hat Trick Productions Ltd

10 Livonia Street, London W1V 3PH. Tel: (020) 7434 2451

Contact: Denise O'Donaghue
Specialises in situation comedy and drama comedy. Sitcoms include *The Peter Principal, Father Ted* and *Drop the Dead Donkey*. Drama includes *Mr White goes to Westminster* and *Crossing the Floor*. Will look at ideas in any form, but prefers a full script. 'Too many promising outlines turn into disappointing scripts'. Will help develop potential writing talent, and provide feedback. Looking for ideas for series comedy and comedy dramas that are strong on character and plot.

Mersey Television Ltd
Campus Manor, Childwall Abbey Road, Liverpool L16 0JP. Tel: (0151) 722 9122
Makes *Brookside* and *Hollyoaks* for Channel 4.

Noel Gay Television
1 Albion Court, Albion Place, Galena Road, London W6 0QT. Tel: (020) 8600 5200
Contact: Anne Mensah
Maker of *Red Dwarf* and *Windrush* and has several associate companies. Will look at unsolicited treatments (one or two pages only) from new writers.

Pearson Television Ltd
1 Stephen Street, London W1P 1PJ. Tel: (020) 7691 6681
Head of Entertainment: Richard Holloway
Head of Comedy: Tony Charles
The UK's largest independent production company. Makes *The Bill*, *Goodnight Sweetheart*, *Birds of a Feather*.

Rose Bay Film Productions
1 Albion Court, Albion Place, London W6 0QT. Tel: (020) 8600 5200
Contacts: Matthew Steiner, Simon Usiskin
Produces for both film and television. An associate company of Noel Gay Television. Says that unsolicited scripts are welcome.

TalkBack Productions
36 Percy Street, London W1P 0LN. Tel: (020) 7323 9777
Contact: Peter Fincham
Specialises in situation comedy and comedy drama. Productions include *Never Mind the Buzzcocks* and *Knowing Me Knowing You*

with Alan Partridge.

Tiger Aspect Productions
5 Soho Square, London W1V 5DE. Tel: (020) 7434 0672, E-mail: *general@tigeraspect.co.uk*
Contact: Charles Brand
Makes *Gimme Gimme Gimme*, *The Thin Blue Line* and *The Vicar of Dibley*. Has a lot of scripted comedy in development. Not interested in unsolicited scripts in the first instance, but will look at short proposals and treatments. Will meet promising writers to discuss ideas. Looking for comedy ideas that are fresh, funny and original – do not send ideas similar to programmes that the company has already made.

United Film and Television Productions
48 Leicester Square, London WC2H 7FB. Tel: (020) 7389 8555
Contact: Tim Vaughan
Productions include *Hornblower* and *Walking on the Moon*.

Wall to Wall Television
8–9 Spring Place, London NW5 3ER. Tel: (020) 7485 7424
Contact: Alex Graham
Output includes *Plotlands*, *It's Not Unusual*, and *A Rather English Marriage*.

Working Title Films
76 Oxford Street, London W1N 9FD. Tel: (020) 7307 3000
Development Executive: Natasha Wharton
TV production has included *Tales of the City*. Not looking for unsolicited scripts but encourages new writing for film through the New Writers' Scheme (contact Natasha Wharton).

World Productions
17 Golden Square, London W1R 4BB. Tel: (020) 7734 3536
Television drama series and serials.

APPROACHING AGENTS

As with independent production companies, agents are private businesses that cannot afford to spend time reading and commenting on scripts that they believe – if only from a cursory look at the subject matter and first page of dialogue – are not going to make it. At the same time, of course, agents need new writers. You are always, therefore, in with a chance.

- Look in *The Writer's Handbook* or the *Writers' and Artists' Year Book* for agents willing to look at scripts or outlines by new writers.
- Give a succinct account of yourself, your ambitions and your circumstances. The agent will want to be assured that you have the determination, as well as talent, to be a full-time professional writer if the opportunity arises.
- Indicate the type of programmes you believe you could write for.
- Make sure your script is laid out in a clear and professional manner.
- ALWAYS enclose a stamped, addressed envelope.

AGENTS' ADDRESSES

Below are some agents who specialise in television work, are interested in new writers, and in some cases are willing to look at unsolicited scripts.

The Agency (London) Ltd

24 Pottery Lane, London W11 4LZ. Tel: (020) 7727 1346. Founded in 1995, The Agency brings together a number of London's most distinguished television agents. Send a preliminary letter describing yourself and outlining your script.

Blake Friedmann Ltd

37–41 Gower Street, London WC1E 6HH. Tel: (020) 7631 4331. Contact for scripts: Julian Friedmann. Will look at unsolicited scripts or outlines.

Peter Bryant (Writers)

94 Adelaide Avenue, London SE4 1YT. Tel: (020) 8691 9085. Interested in sitcoms. Essential that you include return postage with your script or outline.

Casarotto Ramsay Ltd

National House, 60–66 Wardour Street, London W1V 3HP. Tel: (020) 7287 4450. E-mail: *agents@casarotto.uk.com*. Send a preliminary letter describing yourself and outlining your script.

Elspeth Cochrane Agency

11–13 Orlando Road, London SW4 0LE. Tel: (020) 7622 0314. Interested in television drama. Send a preliminary letter describing yourself and outlining your script.

Curtis Brown Ltd

Haymarket House, 28–29 Haymarket, London SW1Y 4SP. Tel: (020) 7396 6600. One of the biggest and most respected agencies, handling television scripts of all kinds. Send a preliminary letter describing yourself and outlining your script.

Eddison Pearson

44 Inverness Terrace, London W2 3JA. Tel: (020) 7727 9113. E-mail: *box1@eddisonpearson.com*. Unsolicited scripts are welcome, but if very long, send sample pages and a letter in the first instance.

Jill Foster Ltd

9 Barb Mews, Brook Green, London W6 7PA. Tel: (020) 7602 1263. Particularly interested in TV comedy and drama. Send a preliminary letter describing yourself and outlining your script.

David Higham Associates Ltd

5–8 Lower John Street, Golden Square, London W1R 4HA. Tel: (020) 7437 7888. Contacts for scripts: Elizabeth Cree, Nicky Lund, Georgina Ruffhead or Gemma Hirst. Send a preliminary letter with synopsis in first instance.

Valerie Hoskins Associates

20 Charlotte Street, London W1P 1HJ. Tel: (020) 7637 4490. Contact: Valerie Hoskins or Rebecca Watson. Specialises in film, television and radio. Send a preliminary letter describing yourself and outlining your script.

Barbara Levy Literary Agency

64 Greenhill, Hampstead High Street, London NW3 5TZ. Tel: (020) 7435 9046. Contact: Barbara Levy or John Selby. Asks for an 'informative' preliminary letter.

Andrew Mann
1 Old Compton Street, London W1V 5PH. Tel: (020) 7734 4751. Contact: Anne Dewe, Tina Betts. Send a preliminary letter describing yourself and outlining your script.

Peter Fraser and Dunlop
503–4 The Chambers, Chelsea Harbour, Lots Road, London SW10 0XF. Tel: (020) 7344 1000. Send a preliminary letter describing yourself and outlining your script.

Sheil Land Associates
43 Doughty Street, London WC1N 2LF. Tel: (020) 7405 9351. Send a preliminary letter describing yourself and outlining your script.

Cecily Ware Literary Agency
19C John Spencer Square, London N1 2LZ. Tel: (020) 7359 3787. Contact: Cecily Ware, Gilly Schuster, Warren Sherman. Specialises in film and television scripts. Approach in writing, with an outline.

Further Reading

TV PLAYS

Some are paperbacks currently in print, others can be ordered through libraries.

Plays that might be said to have influenced contemporary television drama are marked:*.

Soldier, Soldier, John Arden (Methuen, 1967). *Soldier, Soldier* was broadcast in 1960; one of the first great television plays by one of Britain's most important playwrights.

*Talking Heads**, Alan Bennett (BBC Books, 1988); *The Writer in Disguise* (Faber and Faber, 1985).

*The Boys from the Blackstuff**, Alan Bleasdale (Granada, 1983); *The Monocled Mutineer**, (Hutchinson, 1986).

*The After Dinner Game**, Malcolm Bradbury (with Christopher Bigsby) (Arrow Books, 1989). Four plays for television.

*Deadhead**, Howard Brenton (Methuen, 1987).

The Last of the Summer Wine, Roy Clarke (BBC Publications 1976).

Churchill and the Generals, Ian Curteis (BBC Publications, 1980); *The Falklands Play**, (Hutchinson, 1987).

Z Cars, Keith Dewhurst (Longman, 1968). Classic scripts, but note that today series drama is shot on location rather than in the studio.

The Long March, A Woman Calling, Ann Devlin (in *Ourselves Alone*, Faber and Faber, 1988).

Hancock's Half Hour, Galton and Simpson (Woburn Press, 1974).

*After Pilkington**, Simon Gray (Methuen, 1987).

All Good Men, Trevor Griffiths (Faber and Faber, 1977).

Abel's Will, Christopher Hampton (Faber and Faber, 1979).

Licking Hitler, David Hare (Faber and Faber, 1978); *Dreams of Leaving**, (Faber and Faber, 1980).

Still Waters, Julia Jones (Longman, 1978).

Episodes from 'The Liver Birds', Carla Lane (in *Situation Comedy*, Studio, 1980).

Solid Geometry, Ian McEwan (in *The Imitation Game: Three Plays for Television*, Cape, 1981).

Collected Television Plays, David Mercer (2 vols, John Calder, 1981).

Juliet Bravo, Paula Milne (Longman, 1983). Compare the scene structure and ratio of studio/OB between a *Juliet Bravo* script and a *Z Cars* by Keith Dewhurst or Alan Plater.

Annie Kenny, Alan Plater (in *Act Three*, Hutchinson, 1979); *Z Cars*, (Longman, 1968).

Pennies From Heaven, Dennis Potter (Quartet Books, 1981). *Waiting for the Boat*, (Faber and Faber, 1984). *The Singing Detective**, (Faber and Faber, 1986).

Bar Mitzvah Boy, The Evacuees, Spend, Spend, Spend, Jack Rosenthal (in *Three Award Winning TV Plays*, Penguin, 1978); *Three Plays*, (Penguin, 1986).

Penda's Fen, David Rudkin (Davis-Poynter, 1975).

Our Day Out, Willy Russell (in *Act One*, Hutchinson, 1979).

Soldiers Talking, Cleanly, Mike Stott (Eyre Methuen, 1978).

The Ballard of Ben Bagot, Peter Terson (in *Scene Scripts Two*, Longman, 1978).

BOOKS ON WRITING TV DRAMA

Hazel: the Making of a TV Series, Manuel Alvaredo and Edward Buscombe (BFI/Latimer, 1978).

The TV/Film Script, Rodney Bennett (Harrap, London, 1976). A director's viewpoint.

British Television Drama, George W. Brandt (editor) (Cambridge University Press, 1981).

Writing Comedy for Television, Brian Cooke (Methuen, 1983).

Debut on Two, Phillippa Giles and Vicky Licorish (editors) (BBC Books, 1990). Writers' viewpoints, including Jeanette Winterson on adaptations and Paul Jackson on comedy, plus a script editor's advice from Roger Gregory, a former senior script editor at BBC Pebble Mill, and eight 15-minute plays that featured in the BBC 2 *Debut* series. The editors say: '*Debut on Two* – both the book and the series – aims to inspire new writing for television.' Valuable reading for new writers.

How Plays are Made, Stuart Griffiths (Heinemann Educational, 1982).

Writing for Television and Radio, Robert Hilliard (Focal Press, 1976).

Writing for Television, Malcom Hulke (A & C Black, 1980). Includes television techniques, plotting, dialogue, with excellent examples. (The example of *Three Into One Won't Go* as a characterisation on page 71 comes from this book.)

Writing for Television, Gerald Kelsey (A & C Black, 1990). Covers plots, formats, story construction, dialogue and characterisation, and includes very useful script excerpts from *Howard's Way*, *Brookside* and the film drama *Sun Child* by Angela Huth.

Writing for the BBC, Norman Longmate (BBC Books, 1989). Tells you all about the BBC script unit, which no longer exists, and lists the many programme slots that do not require scripts from outside sources. More a round-up of the BBC's overall output than a useful guide for the new writer. Devotes more space to radio, and in particular local radio, than to television. Of little use until a revised edition appears.

Screenwriting for Narrative Film and Television, William Miller (Columbus Books, London, 1988). Excellent in-depth study of techniques by American film maker and professor.

The Boys from the Blackstuff – the Making of TV Drama, Bob Millington and Rob Nelson (Comedia/Routledge, 1986).

The Way to Write for Television, Eric Paice (Elm Tree Books, 1981). Very good introduction for new writers.

Ah, Mischief: the Writer and Television, Frank Pike (editor) (Faber, 1982). A number of television dramatists including David Edgar put forward their views on the problems of working in television drama.

Television Drama: an Introduction, David Self (Macmillan, 1984).

Play for Today: The Evolution of Television Drama, Irene Shubik (Davis Poynter, 1975).

The Largest Theatre in the World, Shaun Sutton (BBC Publications, 1982). Shaun Sutton, highly respected former head of BBC Television Drama Group, gives a history of British television drama.

Film Scriptwriting: a Practical Manual, Dwight Swain (Focal Press, 1982).

Writing for Television Today, Arthur Swinson (A & C Black, 1965). Gives an account of television drama in its early days, and studies outstanding television plays like *Soldier, Soldier* by John Arden and *June Evening* by Bill Naughton.

Writing Scripts for Television, Radio and Film, Edgar Willis (Holt, Rinehart and Winston, 1981).

REFERENCE BOOKS

Writers' and Artists' Yearbook (A & C Black) contains general information and lists agents and publishers. It has a section on broadcasting.

The Writers' Handbook edited by Barry Turner (The Macmillan Press), covers markets for radio, film and television scripts.

Index